Minnesota's 50 Greatest Baseball Players

By Jonathan W. Sweet

Published by Brick Pickle Media, LLC, 2019

Published by Brick Pickle Media, LLC, Chaska, MN

<u>www.BrickPickle.com</u>[1]

For more information, email publishing@chaskabooks.com.

Available as an e-book, trade paperback and 50-copy signed edition

---

Also by Jonathan W. Sweet

Minnesota's 50 Greatest Baseball Players: From Town Ball to the Twins

DeForest: A Small-Town Wisconsin History

Watch for more at https://brickpicklemedia.com/.

AUTHOR'S NOTE

This book began with a tour of Target Field in 2012, when I saw pictures of Willie Mays and Ted Williams during their time playing in Minnesota.

Which prompted a question in my mind: Who were the greatest baseball players in Minnesota history?

But not just those who have played at the old Met, Metrodome or Target Field. What if we looked for the greatest players who had ever played for a Minnesota team? There is a long history of great minor league baseball in Minnesota and many legendary players have passed through the state.

I put together the first list in 2013, but continued to unearth more players as I worked on the book. Several of the players included were active – heck, Joe Mauer was a catcher – when I started this effort, but since then have all retired (with the possible exception of the ageless Bartolo Colon).

Many of these players had their greatest fame elsewhere, but at some point called the baseball diamonds of Minnesota home. The players are presented in alphabetical order.

A note on statistics: In many cases, minor league and Negro League statistics are incomplete, but I've done my best to assemble numbers from a variety of sources to try to paint as complete a picture as possible.

With that, please enjoy this unique look at Minnesota's 50 Greatest Baseball Players.

Bob Allison

A Missouri native, Bob Allison spent his entire 13-year career with the Twins and their predecessors, the Washington Senators.

Born July 11, 1934, in Raytown, MO, Allison grew up in the Kansas City suburbs. From a young age, he worked weekends on nearby farms to help his family make ends meet during the Depression and World War II years. Still, he found time to play baseball, joining his first organized team at the age of 11.

When he reached high school, Allison played football, basketball and track because Raytown High had no baseball team. He also continued to play American Legion baseball. Although his dream was still to play baseball, he accepted a football scholarship from the University of Kansas when he graduated from high school in 1952.

Major league scouts who had been following him since his sandlot days continued to pay attention to him even after he started college. With numerous offers in hand, Allison opted to sign with the Senators in 1955, figuring the woeful team would give him a better chance to make the majors.

He got off to a less-than-impressive start to his minor league career, struggling in his first two seasons. He hit .256 with only five home runs for Class B Hagerstown in 1955 and followed that with a .233 season at Class Charlotte in 1956. That 1956 season, though, did mark the first time he would play on the same team as future Senators and Twins teammate Harmon Killebrew, with whom he would form the core of the lineup in just a few years.

Things didn't get much better at Class AA Chattanooga in 1957, as Allison hit just .246 with two home runs. He and Killebrew were both invited to the Senators' major league camp in 1958, but only Killebrew made the team out of spring training.

Allison finally seemed to turn a corner that year, though, hitting .307 with nine home runs and 93 RBI to earn himself a September call up to the Senators. He hit .200 in 11 games at the end of the season, but showed enough to make the big-league club to start the 1959 season.

He captured the AL Rookie of the Year award that year, even garnering some MVP votes, as he batted .261 and smashed 30 home runs. It was also his first of three trips to the All-Star Game.

He enjoyed arguably his two greatest seasons in 1963 and 1964. In 1963, he batted .271 with 35 home runs and 91 RBI. His 99 runs and his .911 OPS led the American League. He followed that with another All-Star season in 1964, hitting at a .287 clip with 32 HR, 86 RBI and a .957 OPS.

Allison was also a member of the 1965 American League champs and 1969 and 1970 AL West champion clubs, but struggled all three years. His career postseason stats included a .077 average with 1 home run and 3 RBI.

He retired after the 1970 season with a career .255 batting average and an OPS of .829. His 256 career home runs currently rank third all-time for the Twins.

After his retirement, Allison was diagnosed in 1989 with a neurological disease known as Olivo-Ponto cerebellar atrophy or OPCA. In 1990, he helped found the University of Minnesota's Bob Allison Ataxia Research Center. He died from complications of the disease in 1995 at the age of 60. Following his death, the Minnesota Twins created the Bob Allison award to recognize a Twins player who "exemplifies determination, hustle, tenacity, competitive spirit, and leadership both on and off the field."

Allison was named a member of the Twins 40th Anniversary All-Time Team in 2001 and was elected to the Twins Hall of Fame in 2003.

David Bancroft

SS, Duluth White Sox (1909)
Manager, Minneapolis Millers (1933)
Manager, St. Cloud Rox (1947)

B orn in Sioux City, IA, Dave Bancroft moved as a child to Superior, WI. He made his professional debut across the lake for the Duluth White Sox of the Minnesota-Wisconsin League in 1909.

After two more seasons in the league – and three seasons with Portland of the Pacific Coast League – Bancroft joined the Philadelphia Phillies for the 1915 campaign.

In his rookie season, the Phillies made it to the World Series, losing to the Boston Red Sox. For the season, Bancroft finished second in the National League in walks, third in runs scored and sixth in home runs (with 7!).

Bancroft gained the most attention, though, for his fielding skills. Many of his contemporaries considered him to be the greatest fielding shortstop in the game and one of the best of all time.

In 1920, he was traded to the New York Giants, where he would be part of the team's 1921 and 1922 World Series championship teams. After Bancroft struggled in 1923, the Giants traded him to the Boston Braves where he would serve as player/manager from 1924 to 1927.

Released after the 1927 season, he would play for the Brooklyn Robins for two years before finishing his playing career in 1930 with the Giants. After two years as a coach for the Giants, he returned to Minnesota to manage the Minneapolis Millers in 1933, guiding the team to a second-place finish.

He would go on to coach and manage in various leagues for the next several years (including a season in 1947 with the St. Cloud Rox) before settling in Superior for the rest of his life.

Bancroft was elected to the National Baseball Hall of Fame by the Veterans Committee in 1971, and died in Superior in 1972.

Earl Battey

C, Minnesota Twins (1961-67)

E arl Battey spent only seven seasons in Minnesota, but was easily the best catcher to play for the Twins until a certain No. 7 came along.

Born January 5, 1935, in Los Angeles, Battey attended Jordan High School in the Watts neighborhood. He was signed by the Chicago White Sox as an amateur free agent in 1953. He spent the next several years bouncing back and forth between the minor leagues and majors, making his big-league debut on September 10, 1955.

He spent the first five seasons of his major-league career as a part-time player, never playing in more than 48 games in a season. But when the Sox traded him to the Washington Senators in 1960 for All-Star first baseman Roy Sievers, he truly blossomed. In that first season, he hit .270 with 15 home runs and 60 RBI and won his first Gold Glove.

Battey continued to excel when the team relocated to Minnesota in 1961. He posted a career-high .302 average that season, with 17 home runs and a second Gold Glove. He added his third-straight Gold Glove in 1962, while also being named an All-Star for the first time.

1963 was another All-Star season, as Battey hit .285 with career highs in home runs (26) and RBI (84). He missed getting named to the All-Star Game in 1964, but made the team again in 1965 and 1966. In 1965, he was one of four Twins to finish in the Top 10 in voting for the American League MVP award as the Twins advanced to the World Series.

Nagging injuries caught up with Battey by 1967, and he retired at the age of 33.

In his eight years with the franchise, Battey hit .277, with a .354 OBP and .766 OPS. He led all American League catchers in putouts, assists, caught stealing percentage and many other defensive categories multiple times. Only Joe Mauer has played more games at catcher for the Twins than Battey.

After Battey retired, he moved to New York and worked with at-risk youth. In 1980, he enrolled at Bethune-Cookman University to earn a college degree – and serve as coach for the university's baseball team. After completing his education, he became a high school teacher and baseball coach in Ocala, FL.

He was named a member of the Twins 40th Anniversary All-Time Team in 2001. Battey died in 2003 and was posthumously elected to the Twins Hall of Fame in 2004.

Don Baylor

DH, Minnesota Twins (1987)

Don Baylor's 27 games in Minnesota was easily the shortest stint of any of his major league stops, but he made a big impact on the 1987 World Champion Twins – and the Twins made a significant impact on him as well.

"It was the best time I ever had in the game, playing with these guys right here," Baylor said of the 1987 team in an interview with the *St. Paul Pioneer Press* in 2007, while in town to celebrate the 20th anniversary of the 1987 title.

"I wasn't (in Minnesota) a long time, just two months," Baylor told the paper. "But all of a sudden you develop a chemistry when you go through things like that."

Baylor joined the Twins for the final month of the 1987 season after Minnesota acquired him from the Boston Red Sox on September 1. In 20 games during the regular season, he hit .286, with a .397 OBP, and was credited with providing an important veteran presence during the pennant race and postseason.

He batted .400 in the American League Championship Series against the Detroit Tigers. In the World Series against the St. Louis Cardinals, he hit .385 with a key two-run home run in Game 6 off of John Tudor to tie the game at 5-5 as the Twins faced elimination.

Baylor would play one more season, for the Oakland Athletics in 1988, making his third straight World Series appearance (starting in 1986 with the Boston Red Sox), before retiring after 19 seasons in the major leagues.

Over the course of those 19 years, Baylor would bat .260, with 2,135 hits, 338 home runs, 1,276 RBI and an OPS of .777 with the Baltimore Orioles, Athletics, California Angels, New York Yankees, Red Sox and Twins. He was a three-time winner of the Silver Slugger award, in 1983, 1985 and 1986. He was also hit by a pitch 267 times during his career, which was the modern record until Craig Biggio passed him in 2005.

His 1979 season was a career year, as he batted .286 with a league-leading 139 RBI and 120 runs for the Angels. He also hit a career-high 36 home runs on his way to winning the American League MVP award.

After his playing career ended, Baylor was the hitting coach for the Milwaukee Brewers in 1990 and 1991. He spent the 1992 season in the same position for the St. Louis Cardinals before being named as the first manager of the Colorado Rockies in 1993.

In 1995, Baylor managed the Rockies to their first postseason berth as they won the National League Wild Card and Baylor was named the National League Manager of the Year. After the Rockies fired him following the 1998 season, Baylor spent a season as the hitting coach for the Atlanta Braves. Baylor was the manager of the Chicago Cubs from 2000 to 2002, and then held coaching positions with the New York Mets, Seattle Mariners, Rockies, Arizona Diamondbacks and Los Angeles Angels of Anaheim.

Baylor died of multiple myeloma, a cancer that attacks the bone marrow, in 2017.

Bert Blyleven

P, Minnesota Twins (1970-76, 1985-88)

Rik Aalbert Blyleven spent half his 22-year career in Minnesota, starting out with the Twins as a 19-year-old rookie in 1970. He enjoyed his only 20-win season as a member of the team in 1973 and claimed 149 of his 287 career wins during his two stints in a Twins uniform.

Blyleven was born April 6, 1951, in the Netherlands. His family moved to Canada when he was two years old and then California when he was five. After playing at Santiago High School, Blyleven was drafted by the Minnesota Twins in the third round of the 1969 draft.

After only 28 games in the minor leagues, Blyleven made his major league debut in 1970 at the age of 19. He finished 10-9 in 25 starts that season, the first of 10 straight double-digit win seasons for Blyleven. Blyleven won 20 games for the only time in 1973, while also leading the league with nine shutouts and earning his first All-Star selection.

In 1976, vocally unhappy with his salary, Blyleven was traded to the Texas Rangers for Roy Smalley, three other players and cash. In his final start with the Rangers, in 1977, Blyleven pitched a no-hitter. The team traded him to the Pittsburgh Pirates after the 1977 season. In Pittsburgh, he won a World Series in 1979, but eventually became unhappy with the Pirates.

Blyleven had a strong first season in Cleveland in 1981, but missed much of the 1982 and 1983 seasons as he struggled with injuries. The 1984 season saw Blyleven have his best season in years, finishing 19-7 with a 2.87 ERA, and coming in third in voting for the Cy Young award. The Indians traded Blyleven back to the Twins midway through the 1985 season. He won 17 games between the two teams, again finishing third in Cy Young voting. His 25 complete games, five shutouts and 293 2/3 innings pitched all led the league.

He again led the league in innings pitched while winning 17 games for the 1986 Twins. His 50 home runs surrendered were also tops in the baseball. As the Twins advanced to the World Series in 1987, Blyleven won 15 games, but again gave up more home tuns (46) than any other pitcher.

After a subpar 1988 season, the Twins traded Blyleven to the California Angels. He won 17 games in his first season with the Angels, but only eight games in 1990 before missing the 1991 season following rotator cuff surgery. After finishing 8-12 in 1992 season, he signed a free agent contract with the Twins in a 1993 comeback attempt, but failed to make the team out of spring training.

Although he did win two World Series rings, his many years playing for sub-.500 teams probably cost him membership in the elusive 300-win club. He posted a career 3.31 ERA and his 3,701 strikeouts rank 5th all time. He also went 5-1 in six career postseason starts. He was widely regarded as having one of the most devastating curveballs in baseball during his time in the game.

Only Jim Kaat won more games as a Twin. Blyleven ranks first in team history in strikeouts, first in complete games, second in innings pitched and shutouts and third in games started. He was also a member of the Twins 40th Anniversary All-Time Team and the team's All-Metrodome Team.

After a long wait, Blyleven was elected to the Hall of Fame in 2011, his 14th year on the ballot. His No. 28 has been retired by the Twins and he was elected to the team's Hall of Fame in 2002. He has also enjoyed a second career as a popular broadcaster for the team, known for his use of the telestrator to circle fans in the stands, leading to the popular "Circle Me Bert" signs.

Lou Brock

OF, St. Cloud Rox (1961)

Speedster Lou Brock spent his lone minor league season playing for the Rox, a Northern League affiliate of the Chicago Cubs. Statistics are incomplete, but he reportedly batted .361 that season with 33 doubles, six triples and 14 home runs in 128 games. He led the league in batting average, hits (181) and total bases (268) – but not stolen bases.

By the end of the season, the Hall of Famer would make his Cubs debut with a brief four-game stint. Besides that cup of coffee, he played two more seasons and part of a third with the Cubs before he was famously traded to the St. Louis Cardinals for Ernie Broglio.

As a member of the Redbirds, he went on to appear in six All Star Games. He led the National League in stolen bases eight times, including a then-record 118 in 1974. In 1967, he was the first player to steal 50 bases and hit 20 home runs in the same season.

He retired with 938 steals, a record that stood until surpassed by Rickey Henderson. He notched 3,023 career hits and finished with a .293 career batting average and .343 OBP. He batted .391 with 14 steals in three World Series with the Cardinals, winning in 1964 and 1967.

Brock was also the first player to bat in a regular season major league game in Canada when he lined out to start the April 14, 1969, game against the Montreal Expos.

In 1974, the Sporting News named him Major League Player of the Year. He won the Roberto Clemente Award, which recognizes sportsmanship and community service, in 1975. In 1979, he was the National League's Comeback Player of the Year.

Brock was elected to the Hall of Fame in 1985, his first year of eligibility. The Sporting News ranked him No. 58 on its list of Baseball's

100 Greatest Players in 1998. He remains active in the St. Louis community and works with the Cardinals as a special instructor.

Roy Campanella

R oy Campanella signed his first professional contract at age 15 and went on to star for the Baltimore Elite Giants of the Negro National League. Incomplete statistics show he finished his Negro Leagues career with a .314 batting average and .481 slugging percentage.

In 1946, Campanella signed with the Brooklyn Dodgers, one of five black players the Dodgers signed that year, including Jackie Robinson. Robinson would break the color barrier in 1947 when he joined the Dodgers. Hall of Fame and Negro League Legend Monte Irvin wrote in his book, *Few and Chosen*, that if it had been up to him Campanella would have been the first black player in the major leagues.

After two years in the minor leagues, Campanella started the 1948 season with the Dodgers – but as an outfielder. After a month with the big league club, he was sent down to the Saints on May 18, 1948, breaking the color barrier as the first black player in the American Association.

In his book, *It's Good to Be Alive*, Campanella wrote about how that move to St. Paul came about as Dodgers GM Branch Rickey wanted to integrate the American Association.

> *"I know you can make the Dodgers as a catcher," [Rickey] said, "but I want you to help me do something, something very important to me, to you, and to all baseball. I want you to become the first colored ballplayer in the American Association. Do you want to do this?"*

Campanella reluctantly agreed to the plan: "If you want me at St. Paul, that's where I'll play. Because it's in my contract. For no other reason."

When he arrived in St. Paul, he ended up playing for future Dodgers skipper Walter Alston, who had also managed him during an earlier minor league stop in Nashua, N.H.

Campanella got off to a slow start for the Saints, going hitless in his May 22 debut and struggling through his first several games during an East Coast road trip. His stay with the team was brief, though, as he started to dominate the AAA league upon his return to the Twin Cities.

He hit two home runs against the Minneapolis Millers on May 30. The next day, he made his Lexington Park debut, hitting a triple and a home run, driving in three runs.

By July, Campanella was back in Brooklyn, where he would spend the rest of his major league career. In only six weeks with the Saints, he hit .325 with a .432 on-base percentage and .715 slugging average. He hit 13 home runs and had 39 RBI in those 35 games. And his son, Roy Jr., was born in St. Paul on June 20, 1948.

Campanella would go on to have a stellar 10-year career with the Dodgers. In his first full season of 1949, he would hit .287 with 22 home runs and 82 RBI, and make his first of what would be eight straight All-Star Games.

In 1951, he won the first of three MVP awards on the strength of his .325 average, 33 home runs and 108 RBI. He earned his second MVP award with probably his greatest season in 1953, when he hit 41 HRs and knocked in 142 runs. He'd win a third MVP award in 1955.

After the 1957 season, the Dodgers announced their plans to move to Los Angeles. Unfortunately, Campanella never got a chance to play in California after being paralyzed in a car accident in January 1958.

While driving home from the liquor store he operated in Harlem, Campanella hit a patch of ice at an S-curve near his home in Glen Cove, NY, on the north shore of Long Island. The accident left Campanella paralyzed from the shoulders down. Although he eventually regained use of his arms and hands, he required a wheelchair for mobility for the remainder of his life.

He finished his career with a .276 batting average, .360 on-base percentage and .500 slugging percentage. He hit 242 home runs with 856 RBI. Campanella was elected to the Baseball Hall of Fame in 1969. In 1972, the Dodgers retired his No. 39.

Campanella died at the age of 71 in 1993. In 1998, he was ranked No. 50 on *The Sporting News* list of the 100 Greatest Baseball Players. He was also featured on a U.S. postage stamp in 2006, as part of a series honoring baseball sluggers.

Rod Carew

R od Carew spent 12 of his 19 years in the major leagues playing for the Twins.

After playing semi-pro baseball with the Bronx Cavaliers, Carew signed with the Twins in 1964. He joined the Melbourne Twins of the Cocoa Rookie League for the final 37 games of the season. After two seasons in A ball, Carew joined the parent club out of spring training in 1967, making his major league debut on April 11.

Carew made an immediate impact, hitting .292 with a .341 on-base percentage in his rookie year. He captured the AL Rookie of the Year Award, and made the first of 18 consecutive All-Star game appearances.

In 1969, he won the first of seven batting titles, hitting .332 with a .386 on-base percentage and 30 doubles. He also stole home seven times that year, tying a major league record. It was also the first of 15 consecutive seasons Carew hit over .300.

Carew would lead the American League in batting for four straight seasons, from 1972 to 1975. He also led the league in hits in 1973 and 1974 and triples in 1973.

Still, he topped those years with his great 1977 season. Carew won his only MVP award that year after spending most of the season chasing a .400 average, finishing at .388, the highest average since Ted Williams hit .388 in 1957. He also led the league in hits (239), runs (128), triples (16) and on-base percentage (.449).

He would win one more batting title in 1978 for the Twins. After the 1978 season, Carew announced his intention to leave the Twins. The Twins subsequently traded him to the California Angels. He would play seven more seasons there.

On Aug. 4, 1985, Carew got his 3,000[th] hit, ironically against the Twins' Frank Viola. Carew retired after the 1985 season when he received no offers in free agency. In 1995, Carew was among a group of players that received damages when arbitrator Thomas Roberts ruled that the owners had violated baseball's collusion rules.

He finished his Twins career with a .334 batting average and .393 on-base percentage, both the best in franchise history. His 2,085 hits are good for third in Twins history. For his career, he batted .328 with 3,053 hits.

In 1987, the Twins retired his No. 29 – at the first major league baseball game attended by the author, incidentally.

Carew was elected to the National Baseball Hall of Fame in his first year of eligibility in 1990. He worked as the hitting coach for both the Angels and the Milwaukee Brewers, and as a roving instructor for the Twins after his retirement.

He was ranked No. 61 on The Sporting News' list of the 100 Greatest Baseball Players in 1998 and in 2000 he was part of the inaugural class for the Twins Hall of Fame. He was named to the Twins 40th Anniversary All-Time Team in 2001.

Carew was named the second baseman on the Major League Baseball Latino Legends Team in 2005, and in 2016 the American League batting championship trophy was named the Rod Carew American League Batting Championship Award.

Steve Carlton

P, Minnesota Twins (1987-88)

S teve Carlton was one of the greatest pitchers of all time, winning 329 games and racking up more than 4,000 strikeouts. Unfortunately for Twins fans, by the time Lefty got to Minnesota his best days were well behind him.

The Twins acquired Carlton from the Cleveland Indians in July 1987. He would make nine appearances (seven starts) and finish with a 1-5 record and 6.70 ERA. Carlton did earn his third World Series ring that year, but was left off the postseason roster for the Twins. He returned to the Twins in 1988, but was released after only one month and four appearances with an 0-1 record and 16.76 ERA.

But his Twins output was hardly representative of his career. His 329 wins are the 11th most in baseball history – and behind only the great Walter Johnson among lefthanders. His 4,136 strikeouts are the fourth most all time, and he was the all-time leader several times during the 1980s as he and Nolan Ryan dueled for the title. He was also the first pitcher to win four Cy Young awards.

Born and raised in Miami, Carlton signed with the St. Louis Cardinals out of Miami-Dade College in 1963 for a $5,000 signing bonus. He debuted with the Cardinals in 1965. In 1968, he made the first of his 10 All-Star Game appearances. He followed that with All-Star seasons in 1969 and 1971, when he won 20 games for the first time, finishing 20-9.

After a salary dispute, the Cardinals traded Carlton to the Philadelphia Phillies before the 1972 season. It was in Philadelphia where he would go on to have his greatest success.

In 1972, he went 27-10, with a 1.97 ERA for a last-place team that won only 59 games. That earned him the first of his four Cy Young awards and another All-Star appearance. He would play for the Phillies through 1986, winning Cy Young awards in 1977, 1980 and 1982, and making six more All-Star teams.

As late as September 4, 1984, he held the lead in the all-time strike-out race with Ryan, 3,857 to 3,854. Ryan pulled ahead for good by the end of the 1984 season, and an injury-plagued 1985 campaign put Carlton even further behind.

After starting the 1986 season 4-8 with a 6.18 ERA, Carlton was released by the Phillies in June. On July 4, he signed with the San Francisco Giants. He made six starts for the Giants, going 1-3 with a 5.10 ERA, although he did record his 4,000th strikeout with the team before being released.

He finished the season with the Chicago White Sox, then signed with the Indians before the 1987 season. After his 1988 release by the Twins, he attempted to continue pitching but found no takers.

The Phillies retired Carlton's No. 32 in 1989. He was elected to the Hall of Fame in 1994, his first year of eligibility, with 96 percent of the vote. In 1998, *The Sporting News* ranked him No. 30 on its list of the 100 Greatest Baseball Players of the 20th Century.

Orlando Cepeda

1B/OF, St. Cloud Rox (1956); Minneapolis Millers (1957)

F uture Hall of Famer Orlando Cepeda played the bulk of his minor league career in Minnesota after signing with the New York Giants following a tryout in 1955.

After stops in Salem, VA, and Kokomo, IN, Cepeda joined the St. Cloud Rox of the Northern League in 1956. He quickly made an impact, winning the league's triple crown in his single season in St. Cloud. In 125 games, Cepeda batted .355, with a .613 slugging average. He slugged 26 home runs with 112 RBI, 33 doubles and 9 triples.

"I love St. Cloud," Cepeda told the *St. Cloud Times* in 2015. "I had some great days there, great times."

Not only was Cepeda successful on the field, his off-the-field experience was much improved after dealing with segregated facilities and Jim Crow laws during his 1955 season.

"The year before, I went through some tough times ... because I was Latino. I was black," he told the paper. "In St. Cloud, people were very good to me." Cepeda admitted he could have done without the cold early-season weather: "I've never been so cold in my life."

After playing in the Puerto Rican Professional Baseball League that winter, Cepeda spent the 1957 season with the Minneapolis Millers of the American Association. In 151 games, Cepeda hit .309, with 31 doubles, 25 home runs and 108 RBI, finishing in the top 10 in many offensive categories.

With successful seasons in Minnesota under his belt, Cepeda joined the Giants in 1958 for their first season in San Francisco. He was a success from the start, setting a National League rookie record (broken by Albert Pujols in 2001) with 13 home runs through the end of May. For the season, he would hit .312, with 25 home runs and 96 RBI, while his 38 doubles led the National League.

His strong season earned him a unanimous selection as the Rookie of the Year, only the second player (after Frank Robinson) to receive a unanimous vote. A reader poll in the *San Francisco Examiner* also voted him the "Most Valuable Giant" that year. He finished ninth in the voting for National League MVP.

Cepeda went on to have several more successful seasons in San Francisco, making the All-Star game every season from 1959 to 1964. In 1961, he posted what was probably his greatest offensive season, when he hit .311 with a .970 OPS and led the league in home runs (46) and RBI (142). That was good enough to finish second in the National League MVP voting, losing out to Cincinnati's Frank Robinson.

After the 1962 season, he again played in the Puerto Rican Professional Baseball League, where he hurt his knee, an injury that would plague him for the rest of his career. Despite the injury, he had strong seasons in 1963 and 1964 as he played through the pain. The injury finally caught up with him in 1965, as he missed most of the season, making only 40 plate appearances.

He returned to the Giants in 1966, but was traded to the St. Louis Cardinals after playing in only 19 games. In 123 games with Cardinals that season, Cepeda batted .303 with 17 home runs, 58 RBI and 24 doubles. His successful rebound won him the National League Comeback Player of the Year award.

The 1967 season was one of Cepeda's most successful, as he batted a career-high .325 with 25 home runs, a league-leading 111 RBI and 37 doubles, with a .923 OPS. In July, he was named to the National League All-Star team for the seventh and final time in his career. With the Cardinals in the midst of a pennant race, Cepeda won the Player of the Month award in August, when he batted .352 with 5 home runs and 25 RBI.

Cepeda was a unanimous selection as the National League MVP, only the second in league history after Carl Hubbell in 1936. The Cardinals would go on to win the pennant and defeat the Boston Red Sox in seven games to win the World Series, the only championship for Cepeda during his 17-year career.

The Cardinals returned to the World Series in 1968, losing to the Tigers in seven games, but Cepeda's production fell off in what was known as "The Year of the Pitcher," as he managed only a .248 average and .685 OPS, with 16 home runs and 73 RBI.

The Cardinals traded Cepeda to the Atlanta Braves for Joe Torre before the 1969 season. He would play parts of four seasons for the Braves before they traded him to Oakland Athletics for Denny Mc-Clain in July 1972 as his knee injuries worsened. He only appeared in three games for the A's before they released him.

Intending to retire, he opted to sign with the Boston Red Sox for the 1973 season when they offered him the newly created designated hitter role for the team. He was named Designated Hitter of the Year, batting .289 with 20 home runs, 25 doubles and 86 RBI. His 20-home run season made him the first player to hit 20 home runs with four different teams. He finished his career in 1974 in a part-time role for the Kansas City Royals, hitting .215 in 33 games.

In 1999, he was voted into the Baseball Hall of Fame by the Veteran's Committee, joining Roberto Clemente as the second Puerto Rican in the Hall. That same year, the Giants retired his No. 30. In 2008, the Giants unveiled a life-sized bronze statue of Cepeda outside of AT&T Park, making him the fourth player so honored by the club.

Jimmy Collins

3B, Minneapolis Millers (1909)

By the time Jimmy Collins arrived in Minneapolis in 1909, he was near the end of his Hall of Fame career.

Millers owner Mike Cantillon brought Collins to Nicollet Park to play third base and manage the team. Although the team contended for much of the season, they slumped at the end of the year, finishing in third place. As a player, Collins hit .273 with 21 doubles in 153 games in his sole season in Minneapolis.

But before coming to Minneapolis, Collins had a successful, 14-year major league career. Playing in the Deadball Era, Collins was considered the greatest third basemen of his era and is widely regarded as a pioneer for the modern defensive play of the position.

Collins was born Jan. 16, 1870, in Niagara Falls, N.Y., but his family soon moved to Buffalo, N.Y. It was there that Collins honed his baseball skills playing for local amateur teams. After graduating from high school in 1888, Collins took a job as a clerk with the Delaware, Lackawanna and Western Railroad. He continued to play amateur ball and in May 1893 was offered a chance to play for the Buffalo Bisons of the Eastern League.

After he played two seasons with Buffalo, the Boston Beaneaters of the National League paid $500 to acquire his rights. He made his debut with the club in 1895, but after 11 games as an outfielder was loaned to another National League club, the Louisville Colonels. It was in Louisville that he made his debut as a third baseman. His success there prompted the Beaneaters to try to get him back, and he rejoined the team in 1896.

By 1897, Collins was firmly entrenched as the Boston third baseman, established as a leading defender. He hit .346 that year with 132 RBI. He continued to excel the next season, hitting .328 with 111 RBI and a league-leading 15 home runs in 1898. The Beaneaters won the

National League pennant both years, but Collins continued to clash with ownership over his salary.

That continued tension prompted Collins to leave the Beaneaters after the 1900 season, jumping to the Boston Americans of the new American League for the 1901 season. Collins would not only be playing third base for the new team, but also serving as the manager. Besides a big raise, Collins was also given ownership shares in the team that would eventually become the Red Sox.

He continued to excel as a player, hitting .332 his first season with the Americans, leading the team to a second-place finish in 1901. After a third-place finish in 1902, Collins led the team to its first American League pennant in 1903. His club would win the first World Series that fall, topping National League champion Pittsburgh five games to three in the best-of-nine series.

The Americans repeated as American League champions in 1904, but there was no World Series as the National League pennant-winning New York Giants refused to play the Boston team.

In 1905, the team finished in fourth place as Collins clashed with new owner John I. Taylor over personnel issues. Taylor left the country for a six-month European trip in 1906 and Collins was named the team president, while continuing to play and manage the team. By July 1, though, the whole thing had fallen apart with Collins announcing he was leaving the team.

After Collins failed in efforts to buy another baseball team, he asked to return to the Americans. The team brought him back in 1907, but as a player only. After only 41 games, he was traded to the Philadelphia Athletics. He played for Philadelphia for the rest of that season and a final season in 1908.

He finished his career with a .294 average and 1,999 hits.

After his one season in Minneapolis, Collins signed on to manage the Providence Grays in October 1909. He lasted a season and a half there before being fired in June 1911.

After retirement, Collins moved back to Buffalo with his wife and children where he would manage his real estate holdings and work for the Buffalo Parks Department. In 1922, he was appointed president of the Buffalo Municipal Baseball Association, a position he would hold until his death, March 6, 1943.

Collins was elected to the National Baseball Hall of Fame in 1945, as the first third baseman to be enshrined.

Bartolo Colon

He's the pitcher that gave every over-the-hill, overweight former athlete something to talk about. Generously listed at 5'11" and 285 lbs. at the end of his career, Bartolo "Big Sexy" Colon didn't look like the elite pitcher he was. "If he can do it, I can do it," countless fans surely said.

Born May 24, 1973, in Altamira, Dominican Republic, Colon grew up harvesting fruit and coffee. He built strength and accuracy throwing rocks at coconuts and mango trees. Between work, he found time to play a few innings with local baseball teams. Word of his exploits eventually found their way to a scout for the Cleveland Indians, who signed the 20-year-old Colon (who they believed to be 18) as a free agent in 1993.

Colon started out with the Rookie-level Burlington Indians of the Appalachian League, pitching 12 games in 1994. He quickly worked his way up the minor-league ranks, playing A-ball in 1995 and at the AA and AAA levels in 1996. He was named the team's Minor League Player of the Year in 1995.

Colon made his major-league debut April 4, 1997, pitching for the Indians against the Anaheim Angels. He split his rookie season between Cleveland and AAA Buffalo, posting a 4-7 record with a 5.65 ERA in 19 games at the major-league level and a 7-1 record and 2.22 ERA in 10 minor-league games. Colon also pitched a no-hitter for the Bisons that year.

In his first full season for the Indians in 1998, Colon earned his first All-Star nod. He finished the year 14-9 with a 3.71 ERA, six complete games, two shutouts and 158 strikeouts in 31 games. Colon continued to be a fixture in the Indians rotation for the next several years, eclipsing double digits in wins every season. In 2000, Colon pitched a one-hitter against the Yankees. Colon also had a 2-2 record with a 2.35 ERA in six postseason starts for the Indians.

With the Indians struggling in 2002, the team traded Colon to the Montreal Expos at the trade deadline. Between the two leagues, Colon won 20 games for the first time, finishing 20-8 with a 2.93 ERA and leading baseball with eight complete games. Colon was the last active player to have played with the Expos. The Expos traded Colon to the Chicago White Sox before the 2003 season. In his lone season with the Sox, Colon again led the majors in complete games with nine.

Colon signed a free agent contract with the Anaheim Angels prior to the 2004 season. He won 18 games that year, and followed that up with a 21-win season in 2005. Colon notched his second All-Star selection that season and won the only Cy Young award of his career. During the playoffs that year, Colon partially tore his rotator cuff. That injury cost him most of the 2006 season as well. He came back to pitch for the Angels in 2007, but struggled to the tune of a 6-8 record and 6.34 ERA.

Colon pitched for the Boston Red Sox in 2008 and White Sox again in 2009 before missing the entire 2010 season with injuries. After a year with the Yankees, Colon signed with the Oakland A's in 2012. He won 10 games that season, but was also suspended for 50 games after testing positive for synthetic testosterone. When he returned in 2013, Colon had his best season in years with an 18-6 record and 2.65 ERA, earning another All-Star bid.

After spending almost his entire career in the American League, Colon moved over to the National League in 2014, signing with the New York Mets. He won 15 games that year, including his 200th career win. That made him just the third Dominican-born pitcher to reach that total. After posting 14 wins in 2015, Colon won 15 in 2016 and made his fourth All-Star team. On May 7, 2016, he hit his first career home run, making the 42-year-old Colon the oldest player to do so.

Colon signed a one-year contract with the Atlanta Braves before the 2017 season, but the team released him after he started the season 2-8 with an 8.14 ERA in 13 starts. That cleared the way for the Twins to add him to their struggling pitching staff.

In 15 starts with the Twins, Colon finished 5-6 with a 5.18 ERA. His August 7 complete game against the Texas Rangers made the 44-year-old the oldest pitcher American League pitcher to hurl a complete game since the 45-year-old Nolan Ryan did so in 1992. On August 20, Colon defeated the Arizona Diamondbacks, making him the 18th pitcher to record a win against every major league team.

Colon joined the Texas Rangers for 2018 and won seven games on the season. His August 7 win over the Seattle Mariners was No. 246 for his career, the most all-time by a Latin American-born pitcher.

As of this writing, Colon has not signed with a team for the 2019 season, but also has yet to announce his retirement. Through 2018, Colon has a 247-188 record, 4.12 ERA, 38 complete games, 13 shutouts and 2,535 strikeouts in 565 games. His wins, strikeouts and games started totals all rank in the Top 50 all time. His 439 home runs surrendered are the seventh-most in major-league history.

Ray Dandridge

3B, Minneapolis Millers (1949-52)

Many consider Ray Dandridge the greatest third basemen to never play in the major leagues. The Negro League star was a great fielder and hitter, but was considered too old by the time baseball integrated.

Dandridge was born Aug. 13, 1913, in Richmond, VA. He played for several local amateur teams before signing with the Negro League's Detroit Stars in 1933 at the age of 19.

He hit only .218 that first season, but really exploded on to the scene in 1934 when he joined the Newark Dodgers (later Eagles). Negro League stats are incomplete, but Dandridge hit over .400 that season. He stayed with the Eagles through the 1938 season, when he left to play in Mexico for Jorge Pasquel.

Dandridge played in Mexico for most of the next decade, with the exception of 1944, when he returned to Newark for one season (and hit .370). He even reportedly turned down a chance to play for Bill Veeck's Cleveland Indians in 1947. Dandridge felt he was being treated well by Pasquel, who was paying him the princely sum of $10,000 a year.

Dandridge returned to the United States in 1949 as player/manager of the New York Cubans. Later that year, the Cubans sold the contracts of Dandridge and pitcher Dave Barnhill to the New York Giants, who assigned him to Minneapolis, its American Association affiliate.

Both players made their debut during a June 5 doubleheader, although Dandridge played in the first game, making him the first black player for the Millers. In 99 games with the Millers that year, Dandridge hit .362 with a .392 OBP. That was good enough for Dandridge to win the league's Rookie of the Year award at the age of 36 (although he told the Giants he was younger).

In 1950, he was an American Association All Star, and he garnered league MVP honors when he hit .311 with 11 home runs, 80 RBI and 106 runs.

He played two more seasons for the Millers, hitting .324 in 1951 and .291 in 1952. In 1951, he served as a mentor to future Hall of Famer Willie Mays during his brief stay with the Millers. In fact, according to Dandridge, he and Mays were together at a movie theater in Sioux Falls, Iowa, when Mays got the news that he was being called up to play for the Giants.

Whether because of his age or his race, despite that success, the Giants never called him up to the major leagues. (Dandridge also suffered appendicitis in 1951, which may have cost him a chance at the big leagues.) For his Millers career, he hit .318 in 501 games.

He played the 1953 season for Oakland and Sacramento of the Pacific Coast League before retiring. He later worked as a scout for the San Francisco Giants and ran a recreation center in Newark, N.J.

Dandridge was elected to the National Baseball Hall of Fame in 1987 and the Mexican Professional Baseball of Fame in 1989. He died in 1994 at the age of 80.

John "Cannonball" Donaldson

Bertha Fishermen (1924-25, 1927)
Lismore Gophers (1926)
St. Cloud Saints (1930)
Fairmont John Donaldson's All Stars (1932)

John Donaldson could quite possibly be the greatest pitcher you've never heard of.

Donaldson played throughout the state of Minnesota in the pre-integration days of baseball, bouncing from Negro League teams to town ball teams to barnstorming teams.

The Donaldson Network, a group of volunteer researchers led by Peter Gorton, has done incredible work uncovering the career of this pitching great. According to their research, the southpaw pitched in 130 Minnesota cities and towns from the 1910s to the 1930s.

The group has documented 399 wins and nearly 5,000 strikeouts for the pitcher that many of his contemporaries considered to be the equal of the legendary Satchel Paige.

Donaldson was born in Missouri in 1892 and reportedly showed an interest in baseball from a very young age, pitching for his school teams in grade school and high school. He made his professional debut in 1911, pitching for the Tennessee Rats barnstorming team and made his first appearance in Minnesota that fall.

In 1912 Donaldson joined the All Nations traveling ballclub owned by J.L. Wilkinson, who later owned the Kansas City Monarchs of the Negro National League. The All Nations team was made up of players of several different nationalities. He would spend six years traveling throughout the United States and Canada with the All Nations team, including dozens of appearances in Minnesota.

The team disbanded in 1917 when many players, including Donaldson, left to serve in World War I. After returning from Europe, Donaldson played for teams in New York, Indianapolis and Detroit. He signed with Wilkinson's Monarchs team in the newly formed Negro National League in 1920.

Donaldson joined his first Minnesota team in 1924, signing with the Bertha Fishermen (named for manager Ernie Fisher) for a salary of $325 per month. The small-town team – Bertha had a population of about 600 people – provided Donaldson a guaranteed contract and was only a short train ride from his wife's family in Minneapolis.

The star proved to be a major attraction, as the Bertha club drew large crowds while playing an independent schedule throughout the Midwest. Home games proved so popular that the team had to expand the bleachers at the local park to make room for spectators.

The Fishermen won both the Central Minnesota and Northwest Minnesota State championships in 1924. Donaldson finished the season with a 21-3 record and more than 300 strikeouts. He also led the team in hitting with a .439 average. His performance earned him a raise to $400 per month for the 1925 season.

That 1925 season proved to be another successful one for Donaldson, as he finished with a 23-5 record and .387 batting average. After the 1925 season, Donaldson played games for several other small-town teams in Minnesota, including the Lismore Gophers.

The Gophers were so impressed with Donaldson that they lured him away from Bertha for the 1926 season with a contract for $450 a month and the use of a furnished house. Unfortunately, the results were subpar as Donaldson suffered from overuse. The Gophers finished the season 20-24, with Donaldson pitching in all but six games.

He returned to Bertha in 1927 and again posted a successful season, with fans packing the stands to see the now-legendary hurler. He pitched his way to a 22-4 record and batted .440 for the season.

Despite that success, Donaldson opted to leave the Fishermen for the 1928 season, signing with a Scobey, Montana, ballclub. When touring in Minnesota, they called themselves John Donaldson's All Stars to play on his draw at the gate. He spent 1929 touring with the Colored

House of David team – officially from Havana, Cuba, but really made up of black players from throughout the United States.

The 38-year-old Donaldson returned to Minnesota to play for the St. Cloud Saints in 1930 then joined the Kansas City Monarchs in 1931. He finished his career in Minnesota in 1932 when he formed an all-black baseball team with its home in Fairmont, dubbed John Donaldson's All Stars. After a couple of months playing in Minnesota, the team left on a barnstorming tour to play in other Midwest states.

Donaldson would play and coach for the Monarchs in the 1930s, where Satchel Paige was among the players on the team. Although he never got to pitch in the major leagues, he worked as a scout for the Chicago White Sox in the 1940s and 1950s and helped sign several former Negro League players.

In 1952, the 60-year-old Donaldson was voted one of the best Negro League players ever in a poll by the Pittsburgh Courier of former players. He died in 1970 in Chicago and was buried in an unmarked grave, but was recognized with a marker in 2004 as part of the Negro Leagues Baseball Grave Marker Project.

Film of Donaldson pitching was uncovered in 2010 and as of this writing is posted online at https://vimeo.com/173608869.

Red Faber

P, Minneapolis Millers (1911)

U rban "Red" Faber's time in Minnesota was just a quick stopover during his minor league career, but the Hall of Fame pitcher went on to play 20 seasons in the major leagues, all for the Chicago White Sox.

Faber was born Sept. 6, 1888, on his family's farm near Cascade, Iowa. When Faber was a young child, the family moved to Cascade, where his father ran a tavern and hotel. Faber's family was apparently well-to-do, and could afford to send Faber to prep schools in Prairie du Chien, WI, and Dubuque, Iowa.

He played a single season of baseball for St. Joseph's College in Dubuque in 1909. His play there and for local semi-pro teams caught the eye of the Class B Dubuque Miners of the Illinois-Indiana-Iowa League. He finished the 1909 season with Dubuque and returned there in 1910 before being signed by the Pittsburgh Pirates.

However, the Pirates didn't use Faber and instead shipped him out to Minneapolis. He pitched in only five games for the Millers, winning one game. Despite that short stint, his time with the Millers drastically shaped his career.

Shortly after arriving in Minneapolis, Faber injured his arm in a long-distance throwing contest. While coming back from that injury, Faber learned the spitball from his teammate Harry Peaster. He would go on to use that spitball to great effect in his major league career.

(A spitball is a now illegal pitch in which the ball is altered with saliva, petroleum jelly or some other substance to add extra motion to the pitch. The pitch was banned from Major League Baseball after the 1920 season, but current pitchers were allowed to continue throwing the pitch, which Faber did until his retirement in 1933.)

After two more seasons in the minor leagues, Faber signed with the White Sox, embarking with the team on a world tour at the end of the

1913 season. He joined the club for good in 1914, splitting his time between the bullpen and rotation, winning 10 games and saving a league-leading four games. (It was a *very* different time!)

He posted his first 20-win season in 1915, finishing with a 24-14, a 2.55 ERA and 21 complete games in a league-leading 50 games. He followed that up with a 17-9 record and 2.02 ERA in 1916.

In 1917, he posted a 16-13 record with a 1.92 ERA as the White Sox advanced to the World Series. Faber pitched in four games in the series against the New York Giants, finishing with a 3-1 record and 2.33 ERA as the Sox defeated the Giants in six games.

Faber pitched in only 11 games in 1918 before signing up to join the U.S. Navy during World War I. He returned to the White Sox in 1919 only to suffer arm trouble and a bout with a severe case of the flu. Those maladies caused him to miss the World Series that year – a World Series that later became infamous after several White Sox players took money from gamblers to throw the series to the Cincinnati Reds.

He rebounded in 1920 to finish 23-13 with a 2.99 ERA and 28 complete games. While the franchise was about to enter its darkest era with the lifetime ban of eight players from the game of baseball, Faber would have the best seasons of his career in the early 1920s. He finished the 1921 season 25-15, leading the league with a 2.48 ERA and 32 complete games. In 1922, he went 21-17, again pacing the American League in ERA (2.81) and complete games (31). He also pitched a league-leading 352 innings.

As the White Sox struggled following the suspensions of those key players, Faber found wins harder to come by for the remainder of his career. Although he wouldn't have another 20-win season, he did pitch 11 more seasons for the Sox. When the team wanted to cut his salary by a third following the 1933 season, Faber tried to find another team to pitch for. When he had no luck in that endeavor, he retired at the age of 44.

He finished his career with a 254-213 record and a 3.15 ERA. His 669 games pitched are the most in White Sox history. His 254 wins, 4,086 innings pitched, 273 complete games and 483 games started are second in White Sox history, while his 1,471 strikeouts are third best for the franchise. His 29 shutouts are No. 4 on the White Sox all-time list.

Following his retirement, Faber served as a coach for the White Sox, as well as working in auto sales and real estate. He worked for the Cook County (IL) Highway Department for several years. He was also among the founders of Baseball Anonymous, a charitable organization that assisted former baseball players who had run into financial or physical problems.

Faber was inducted into the Hall of Fame in 1964. He died in Chicago in 1976 at the age of 88.

Gary Gaetti

3B, Minnesota Twins (1981-90)

From his debut, Gary Gaetti gave Minnesota Twins something to enjoy, as he homered in his first at bat on Sept. 20, 1981. It was the first of 201 home runs Gaetti would hit over ten seasons with the Twins, good for eighth among the Twins all-time leaders.

After his cup of coffee in 1981, Gaetti played his first full season in 1982 as part of the Twins class of 1982 that would form the core of the 1987 World Series team. While he posted only a .230 batting average, he did slug 25 home runs and knock in 84 runs and finished fifth in voting for American League Rookie of the Year.

In 1986, Gaetti won the first of four consecutive Gold Gloves at third base. He probably had what was also his best offensive season, as he hit .287 with 34 home runs and 108 RBI, and an OPS of .865.

He followed that up in 1987 with 31 home runs and 109 RBI as the Twins won their first World Series title. Gaetti hit home runs in his first two postseason at bats that year, on his way to winning the American League Championship Series MVP award. For the postseason, he hit .277 with 3 home runs and 9 RBI.

Gaetti was selected for the American League All-Star team for the first time in 1988, posting his only .300 season, as he hit .301. He was also named to the 1989 All-Star Game.

After the 1990 season, Gaetti signed with the California Angels, following that up with stints with the Kansas City Royals, St. Louis Cardinals and Chicago Cubs before finishing his career with five games for the Boston Red Sox in 2000.

Gaetti later admitted he had some regrets about leaving Minnesota and missing out on the 1991 World Series.

"There were a lot of things that went into that decision," Gaetti told Fox Sports North. "It was real hard leaving there. I went

*through a tough time leaving and then coming back and hav-
ing to play against the Twins. That was no fun, getting booed
out of the stadium, but that's all part of it. Looking back on it,
would I have made the same decision? Probably not."*

Gaetti finished his career with .255 batting average, 2,280 hits,
443 doubles, 360 home runs and 1,341 RBI. He was named to the
Twins 40th Anniversary All-Time Team in 2001 and the Twins All-
Metrodome Team in 2009. He was elected to the Twins Hall of Fame
in 2007.

After his playing days ended, Gaetti coached in the Houston Astros
system and for the Durham Bulls, a Tampa Bay affiliate. In 2011, he was
named the first manager of the Sugar Land Skeeters of the independent
Atlantic League. He managed the Skeeters for six seasons before leaving the team at the end of the 2017 season.

Lefty Gomez

P, St. Paul Saints (1930)

Vernon "Lefty" Gomez put together a Hall of Fame career over 14 big league seasons, mostly with the New York Yankees.

Born Nov. 26, 1908, in Rodeo, Calif., Gomez was the youngest of eight children. He started playing baseball as a teenager and tried out for the San Francisco Seals of the Pacific Coast League shortly before his 15th birthday. The team was impressed – but told him to come back when he had added some weight to his 6' 2", 125-lb. frame.

Despite his father's wish for him to give up baseball and attend college after high school, Gomez secretly played for a local semi-pro team and finally earned that contract offer from the Seals.

Not convinced he was ready for the Pacific Coast League, the Seals farmed him out to the Salt Lake City Bees of the Class C Utah-Idaho League for the 1928 season. Gomez finished the season with a 12-14 record and 3.48 ERA, earning an invite to 1929 spring training with the Seals.

That 1929 season with the Seals, with an 18-11 record and 3.44 ERA, was good enough to catch the eyes of the New York Yankees. The Yankees paid the Seals $35,000 for his rights, and ordered him to a health farm to gain weight before spring training in 1930. During spring training he impressed the Yankees enough to make the club, but did suffer an injury that would come back to haunt him. On March 20, in a game against the Cardinals, he was hit in the mouth by a line drive, ending up needing caps on his front teeth.

Gomez made his big-league debut on April 29, 1930, pitching four innings against the Washington Senators. Gomez was still unable to gain enough weight, and team doctors told the Yankees that he was suffering from infected teeth dating back to the spring training injury. So in June, he had all of his upper teeth removed and replaced with ceramic false ones.

Between the surgery and recovery, Gomez continued to struggle in his rookie season, owning a 2-5 record with a 5.55 ERA in 15 games. On July 25, the Yankees announced they were sending Gomez down to the St. Paul Saints of the American Association.

After getting limited opportunities to play in New York, Gomez got the chance to pitch regularly in Minnesota. He split his time between starting and the bullpen, pitching in 17 games and starting nine. He finished the season 8-4 with a 4.08 ERA. The next season Gomez would be with the Yankees to stay.

1931 was the first of four 20-win seasons by Gomez, as he racked up a 21-9 record with a 2.67 ERA (second in the American League) in 40 games.

The next season, Gomez went 24-7 as the Yankees won their first pennant since 1928. He finished fifth in MVP voting in the days before the Cy Young Award. The Yankees swept the Cubs in the World Series that year. Gomez threw a complete game victory in Game 2, giving up a single run in his only start of the series.

The Yankees and Gomez both slipped a bit in 1933, with New York finishing in second place. Gomez won 16 games, but did have a league-leading 163 strikeouts and was named an All-Star for the first midsummer classic – his first of seven straight years as an All-Star.

Gomez would have his best individual season in 1934, winning the pitching Triple Crown – leading the league in wins (26), ERA (2.33) and strikeouts (158). He lost only five games on the year and had a league-leading 25 complete games and six shutouts. He finished third in MVP voting that season.

After reporting to spring training out of shape in 1935, Gomez struggled that year, finishing 12-15. The Yankees returned to the World Series in 1936, but Gomez won only 13 games as he battled a sore arm for much of the season. He did, however, win both of his World Series starts as the Yankees beat the Giants in six games.

Gomez rebounded in 1937 to win his second Triple Crown, again leading the league in wins (21), ERA (2.33), strikeouts (194) and shutouts (6). His 25 complete games were good for second in the American League. He went 2-0, pitching two complete games, in the Yankees' five-game World Series victory over the Giants.

He won 18 games in 1938 as the Yankees won another World Series, then suffered through an arm injury in 1939 as he won only 12 games. The Yankees beat the Cincinnati Reds in the World Series, but Gomez lasted only an inning in his sole start.

Injuries continued to plague Gomez in 1940, limiting him to a 3-3 record with a 6.59 ERA in only nine games. Gomez bounced back to go 15-5 with a 3.75 ERA in 23 games in 1941. The Yankees once again won the World Series, but Gomez didn't play in the series.

By 1942, it appeared Gomez had lost his fastball. He pitched in only 13 games, finishing with a 6-4 record and 4.28 ERA. The following January, the Yankees released him.

Gomez signed with the Boston Braves before the 1943 season, but never appeared in a game before the team released him in May. Shortly after, he signed with the Washington Senators. He made his lone start on May 30, lasting only 4 2/3 innings and taking the loss against the Chicago White Sox. It was his last major league appearance, although he would stay on the Washington roster until they released him in July.

Gomez finished his career with a 189-102 record, 3.34 ERA, 173 complete games, 28 shutouts and 1,468 strikeouts. He was 6-0 with a 2.86 ERA and four complete games in seven World Series starts.

Classified 4-F by his draft board because of his multiple injuries, Gomez contributed to the war effort by participating in USO tours and working for defense companies. In 1945, he helped form the first Venezuelan professional baseball league and was the first manager of the Cerveceria Caracas.

The Yankees hired him in 1946 to serve as the pitching coach for their top farm team, the Newark Bears. When the manager of the Yankees' Class A Team, the Binghamton Triplets, quit in June, the club asked Gomez to step in. The team finished in last place, 45 ½ games back. He returned to manage the team in 1947, another last-place campaign.

After one season as a roving pitching instructor with the Yankees, Gomez joined Wilson Sporting Goods, where he would spend the next 30 years as one of their top salesmen.

He was elected to the Hall of Fame in 1972. The 1983 All-Star Game was dedicated to Gomez as the last surviving player from the 1933 game. He was honored with a plaque in the Yankees' Monument Park in 1987.

He died of congestive heart failure on February 17, 1989, in Larkspur, Calif. In 1999, he was ranked No. 73 on The Sporting News list of the 100 Greatest Baseball Players.

Jim "Mudcat" Grant

P, Minnesota Twins (1964-67)

Mudcat Grant may have only been a Minnesota Twin for less than four seasons, but he holds a special place in the heart of many Baby Boomer Twins fan as part of a great pitching rotation that also included Jim Kaat, Carlos Pascual and Jim Perry.

That 1965 rotation helped the Twins make it to their first World Series, and Grant was the team leader in wins with his 21-7 record, becoming the first African-American pitcher to win 20 games in the American League.

Grant – born in Lacoochee, FL, in 1935 – grew up in the segregated South. He learned the game of baseball as a batboy for a local semi-pro black team, the Lacoochee Nine Devils.

It wasn't until the summer before his 12th birthday in 1947 that Jackie Robinson joined the Brooklyn Dodgers and became the first black player in the modern major leagues. Despite that, Grant still dreamed of playing big league ball, as he writes in his 2006 book, *The Black Aces*:

> *From the time I was eight or nine I dreamed of playing baseball. Because of the ban on blacks in the Major Leagues I had no expectation that I could play anywhere but the Negro Leagues. But that didn't stop me from dreaming, although it was almost like you weren't allowed to expect that the dream was going to come true.*

By the time he was in his teens, Grant had caught the eyes of scouts for several teams in the newly integrated major leagues. Still, with a dream of being the first in his family to attend college, Grant headed off to Florida A & M University in the fall of 1953 on a partial baseball scholarship. He left school in February 1954, though, to attend the Cleveland Indians camp in Daytona Beach, FL.

The Indians signed him that spring and sent him to their Class C minor league team in Fargo, N.D. He won 21 games for the Fargo-Moorhead Twins and was named the Northern League's Rookie of the Year. Grant continued to move up in the Indians organization, joining the parent club in 1958, as one of a handful of African-American pitchers in the American League.

He made his major league debut on April 17, 1958, starting against the Kansas City Athletics at Cleveland Stadium. He finished that rookie season with a 10-11 record as he moved between the starting rotation and bullpen. He'd continue to put up solid if not spectacular numbers over the next several years for the Indians, making the All-Star team in 1963.

Grant had a rough start to his season in 1964, with a 3-4 record and 5.95 ERA to start the season, easily the worst numbers of his career to that point. On June 16, he came to Cleveland Stadium ready to open up a series against the Minnesota Twins. Instead, he was told to head over to the visitors' clubhouse, where he was immediately welcomed by his new teammates. He pitched his way to an 11-9 record with a 2.82 ERA and 10 complete games in the second half of the 1964 season with the Twins.

That was just the teaser for his career year in 1965, though. As the Twins played their way to the American League pennant, Grant led the league in wins (21), winning percentage (.750) and shutouts (6). He finished sixth in voting for the American League MVP award and made his second American League All-Star team.

"It was definitely special for me," Grant said in a 2017 MLB.com interview. "I didn't know there was never an African-American pitcher who won 20 games in the American League. As the season progressed, I started getting all kinds of mail, and even Howard Cosell called me a couple times when I got to 18 wins. So, it was really special."

Grant also acquitted himself well in the World Series as the Twins lost to the Los Angeles Dodgers. He won two of his three starts, tossing two complete games and hitting a home run in Game 6.

In 1966, Grant finished 13-13 with a 3.25 ERA in 35 starts, in what ended up being his final season as a full-time starter. He'd play one more season in Minnesota before being traded to the Dodgers with Zoilo Versalles in November 1967. He finished his Twins career with a 50-35 record, 3.35 ERA, 36 complete games and 10 shutouts in 129 games. His .588 win percentage as a Twin is fourth-best in team history.

Grant played four more seasons in the major leagues for the Dodgers, Montreal Expos, St. Louis Cardinals, Oakland Athletics and Pittsburgh Pirates before retiring following the 1971 season with 145 wins.

Since his retirement, Grant has worked to recognize "The Black Aces," the 15 African-American pitchers that have won 20 games in a season. In 2006, he published his book *The Black Aces: Baseball's Only African-American Twenty-Game Winners*, recognizing those pitchers as well as standout Negro League pitchers that he feels could have been 20-game winners if given the opportunity to pitch in the Major Leagues.

In 2017, the Twins honored Grant with the Kirby Puckett Alumni Community Service Award.

Kent Hrbek

T he story of Kent Hrbek is that of another local boy made good, but unlike Paul Molitor, Jack Morris or Dave Winfield, Hrbek spent his entire major league career playing for the local nine.

Hrbek was born May 21, 1960, in Minneapolis and grew up in Bloomington, site of Metropolitan Stadium, the home of the Twins and Vikings before they moved into the Metrodome. As a young player, he wore No. 6 in honor of his favorite player, Tony Oliva. Living close enough to ride his bike to the stadium, Hrbek spent plenty of time at the old Met.

Hrbek played his high school ball at Bloomington Kennedy High School, where he caught the eye of Met Stadium concession worker Smokey Teewalt. Teewalt's son played against Hrbek for Bloomington Lincoln and Teewalt told the Twins they should check out that Hrbek kid.

Hrbek signed a letter of intent to play baseball at the University of Minnesota, but was also drafted by the Twins in the 17th round of the 1978 draft. The Twins offered a $5,000 signing bonus, which Hrbek turned down. By the end of the summer, they upped the offer to $30,000 and Hrbek signed with the club.

He signed too late to play that year, but in 1979 made his pro debut for the rookie-level Elizabethton Twins. He suffered a knee injury just a few weeks into the season and ended up batting .203 with 1 home run in 17 games. He came back in 1980 to play A ball for Wisconsin Rapids, where he hit .267 with 19 home runs and 76 RBI. His teammates that year included future Twins 3B Gary Gaetti.

That was good enough for the Twins to move Hrbek up to Visalia to start the 1981 season. In 121 games there, Hrbek hit .379 with an OPS of 1.076, 27 home runs and 111 RBI. That impressed the Twins brass, and allowed Hrbek to make the rare jump from A ball to the major leagues. He made his major league debut on August 21, 1981, at Yankee Stadium. Hrbek wrote about the experience in his 2007 book, *Kent Hrbek's Tales from the Minnesota Twins Dugout*:

> *When I walked onto the field, I was in awe. One second I'm at Visalia playing in a stadium that today I can't even remember the name of, the next thing I'm at Yankee Stadium. ... This was the House that Babe Ruth built. You kind of felt like you were in the place where baseball had been invented.*

If he was nervous, Hrbek didn't show it in that first game, hitting a game-winning home run off of future teammate George Frazier in the 12th inning. Unfortunately, his home debut wasn't quite as successful as he injured his hamstring reaching for a low throw at first base.

Hrbek did come back in September, but as it turned out, that game winner in his debut was Hrbek's only home run that season. Playing in 24 games and making 73 plate appearances, he finished the season with a .239 average.

Hrbek's official rookie season in 1982 garnered him national attention. Hrbek made his first (and only) All Star Game and finished second in Rookie of the Year voting to future Hall of Famer Cal Ripken Jr. The Twins moved into their new home at the Metrodome in 1982, and Hrbek hit the first home run in the new stadium in an exhibition game against the Philadelphia Phillies. For the season, he batted .301 with 23 home runs and 92 RBI.

The team, however, wasn't quite as successful. The Twins finished the first season in their new home with a 60-102 record. It was the first 100-loss season in Twins history (although the Senators had worse seasons) and the Twins worst record until they lost 103 games in 2016.

There was some light on the horizon, though, as Hrbek was joined on the 1982 team by pitcher Frank Viola, catcher Tim Laudner, 3B

Gary Gaetti and outfielders Tom Brunansky and Randy Bush as the core of the 1987 World Series champs started to come together.

After improving by 10 games in 1983, the Twins made their first run at the postseason in more than a decade in 1984. On September 24, the Twins were 81-75, only a half game behind the Kansas City Royals. The team lost its final six games of the season, though, to finish 81-81, three games behind the Royals. For Hrbek, it was arguably his most successful individual season, as he hit .311 with 27 home runs and a career-high 107 RBI. He finished second in balloting for the American League MVP award to Detroit Tigers pitcher Willie Hernandez.

Hrbek continued to play solid ball the next two seasons as the Twins struggled on the field. By 1987, though, both Hrbek and the Twins were ready to make a move.

Hrbek hit .285 with a career-high 34 home runs as the Twins made the postseason for the first time since 1970. With the Twins 85-77 regular-season record, most fans and prognosticators didn't give Minnesota much of a chance in the playoffs. They also had the remarkably bad road record of 29-52, but won a Major League-best 56 home games. Hrbek says the team knew that home field advantage would be important in the playoffs:

> I can still remember the feeling I had walking downstairs to go onto the field for Game 1 of the playoffs. The place was electric. And once the game started, the noise was so incredible it made the hair stand up on the back of your neck.

The Twins would win the World Series that year, although Hrbek struggled, batting only .182 in the playoffs. He did hit two home runs, though, including a grand slam home run in Game 6 that helped seal the Twins win.

For the next several years, Hrbek had what came to be his typical season, hitting 20 to 25 home runs, batting somewhere around .280 and playing strong defense and anchoring the Twins lineup. Hrbek's contract expired after the 1989 season, but despite bigger offers from other teams, he opted to stay with Twins for $14 million over five seasons.

After slipping to last place in 1990, the Twins rebounded in 1991 to finish 95-67 and win the American League West. Hrbek hit 20 home runs, his eighth-straight season with at least 20 home runs, second only to Harmon Killebrew in team history.

Hrbek struggled again in the postseason as the Twins won their second World Series title in five years. He hit only .128, although he did hit a home run in Game 1 of the World Series, a 5-2 Twins win over the Atlanta Braves. Hrbek did, however, cement his place in World Series lore with a controversial play in the Twins Game 2 win.

In the third inning with two outs and Lonnie Smith on first base, Ron Gant singled to left. Smith advanced to third base and when Dan Gladden's throw went past third-baseman Scott Leius, Gant took a large turn at first. Pitcher Kevin Tapani picked up the ball and threw to Hrbek as Gant scrambled back to the bag. Gant reached the base safely standing up but was off-balance as Hrbek took the throw and applied the tag, wrapping his arm around Gant's leg. Both players stumbled backward, and with Hrbek's tag still on him, Gant was called out. The Braves (and their fans) protested that Hrbek had pulled Gant off the bag.

The play is still what he is most known for outside of Minnesota, Hrbek says, noting that he still avoids connecting flights through Atlanta's airport whenever possible. In the wake of the play, Hrbek received hate mail and death threats from Atlanta fans.

During spring training in 1992, Hrbek's daughter, Heidi, was born. That, combined with more injuries and aches and pains prompted Hrbek to begin thinking about retirement.

"I'd be at home and look at the clock and say, 'Oh I've got to go to the park today,'" Hrbek writes in his book. "Before it was always, 'Oh, I get to go to the park today.'"

By 1994, Hrbek knew he was going to finish out his five-year contract and retire at the end of the season. He made it official with an August 4 press conference. When the players went on strike August 11, Hrbek's career was over at the age of 34.

In 14 years with the Twins, Hrbek played in 1,747 games for the team, behind only Harmon Killebrew, Joe Mauer and Kirby Puckett. He finished his career with a .282 average. His 293 home runs and 1,086 RBI are both second to Killebrew. His .481 slugging average and .848 OPS are both third-best in Twins history.

In 1995, the Twins retired his No. 14. He was inducted into the Twins Hall of Fame as part of the inaugural class in 2000. He was also a member of the Twins 40th Anniversary Team and the Twins All-Metrodome Team.

Torii Hunter

OF, Minnesota Twins (1997-2007, 2015)

After the Twins won the World Series in 1991, the '90s didn't give Minnesota fans too much to be excited about.

But as the decade drew to a close, a new crop of young players was starting to emerge. Torii Hunter ended up being the best of this young group that would lead the Twins to several division titles during the 2000s.

Born July 18, 1975, in Pine Bluff, AR, Hunter was one of four brothers in a family that often lived in poverty. With sports as an escape from the prevalent crime and drugs in the area, Hunter played baseball, football, basketball and track. In high school, he was a standout quarterback and safety and garnered headlines in basketball and track. A bit of a late bloomer on the diamond, he eventually became a star in baseball as well.

Hunter was named an all-state outfielder his final two seasons of high school and in 1992 was named to the U.S. Junior Olympic team. With college and pro scouts attending his games, Hunter continued to draw attention. He had a scholarship opportunity from Pepperdine University, but turned down that offer after the Twins drafted him with their first-round pick (No. 20 overall) in the 1993 draft.

Hunter quickly signed with the Twins for a $450,000 signing bonus and had a brief stint with the Rookie-level Elizabethton Twins. In 28 games with the team, he only managed a .190 average.

When he moved up a level in 1994, the results were better. He spent the year with the Class A Fort Wayne Wizards of the Midwest League where he hit .293 with 10 home runs in 91 games. He took a step back in 1995 when he moved up to the High A Fort Myers Miracle, hitting only .246.

Even as he struggled at the plate, Hunter was impressing the Twins with his defense and potential. He spent most of the 1996 and 1997 seasons at AA New Britain. In 1997, he made a brief appearance for the Twins as a pinch runner in one game.

He returned to New Britain to start the 1998 season, but was called back up to Minnesota at the end of April. He notched his first big league hit May 1 and played in a handful of games before heading back down to New Britain. After a successful run there, he was promoted to the AAA Salt Lake Buzz, where he hit .337 in 26 games to finish out the season.

Hunter was one of 10 rookies on the Twins major league roster to start the 1999 season. The young team finished with the worst record in baseball. For his part, Hunter hit .255 in 135 games while playing a stellar center field.

He returned to the Twins to start the 2000 season, but struggled at the plate as the Twins embarked on another last-place season. With an average hovering near the Mendoza line, the Twins sent Hunter down to Salt Lake at the end of May. Hunter tore up the PCL, hitting .368 with 18 home runs and 61 RBI in 55 games. He continued his hot-hitting ways when he returned to the Twins in July, finishing the season with a .280 average. His 12 outfield assists were third in the American League in only 99 games.

The lumps of 1999 and 2000 finally started paying off in 2001, as the Twins got off to a hot start, winning 14 of their first 17 games. The team was still in first place at the All-Star break, but faded down the stretch. Still, the 85-77 record the team posted that the year was the club's first winning record since 1992. Hunter hit .261 with 32 doubles, 27 home runs, 92 RBI and a .784 OPS, all career bests at that point. He racked up 14 outfield assists and won the first of his nine straight Gold Glove awards.

The Twins finally broke through in 2002, winning their first AL Central title. Hunter hit .289 on the season, adding 37 doubles, 29 home runs, 94 RBI and a career-high 23 stolen bases. In his first All-Star Game appearance that summer he made the highlight reels when he made a great catch to steal a home run from Barry Bonds. Hunter finished sixth that season in voting for the American League MVP award.

As the Twins racked up two more division titles in 2003 and 2004, Hunter continued to excel. In 2005, both Hunter and the team struggled. Hunter played in only 98 games after suffering an ankle injury and the Twins fell to third place, finishing 83-79.

The Twins started out slow in 2006 as well, but heated up as the summer went on. Behind the hitting of Hunter, batting champ Joe Mauer and MVP Justin Morneau and the pitching of Cy Young winner Johan Santana, veteran Brad Radke and phenom Francisco Liriano, the Twins roared to 96 wins. Hunter hit .278 with a career-high 31 home runs and 98 RBI. Unfortunately, the postseason results for the Twins were once again disappointing as the team was swept out of the playoffs by the Oakland Athletics.

The Twins fell to third place in 2007, finishing with a 79-83 record, while Hunter had a typical season, hitting .287, a career-high 45 doubles, 28 home runs and a career-high 107 RBI. He earned another All-Star nod and added another Gold Glove. With Hunter a free agent, the Twins opted not to match the offers he was getting from other teams. Hunter signed a five-year, $90 million deal with the Anaheim Angels.

During his five years with the Angels, Hunter continued to put up solid offensive numbers, winning his first Silver Slugger award in 2009. He added two more Gold Glove awards in 2008 and 2009 and was an All-Star in 2009 and 2010. In 2009, Hunter was named as part of the Twins' All-Metrodome team.

Hunter returned to the American League Central in 2013 when he signed a deal with the Detroit Tigers. He made his final All Star team that year and also won his second Silver Slugger award. He hit his 300th career home run in 2013 off of Twins pitcher P.J. Walters.

When Hunter became a free agent after the 2014 season, the Twins brought him back to finish out his career in Minnesota. In his second go-round, Hunter hit .240 with 22 home runs and 81 RBI and was credited with providing a strong veteran clubhouse presence. The team improved to 83-79 in 2015, posting its first winning record since 2010, and staying in the playoff hunt until the final week of the season. After the season ended, Hunter announced his retirement.

Hunter retired with a .277 career average, 498 doubles, 353 home runs, 1,391 RBI and nine Gold Gloves. His 214 home runs as a Twin are the sixth-most in franchise history. He was inducted into the Twins Hall of Fame in 2016.

Monte Irvin

OF, Minneapolis Millers (1955)

One of the great Negro League stars, Monte Irvin was the choice of many players to break baseball's color barrier.

"Monte was the choice of all Negro National and American League club owners to serve as the No. 1 player to join a white major league team," Effa Manley, owner of the Newark Eagles, and fellow Hall of Famer is quoted as saying by the Baseball Hall of Fame. "We all agreed, in meeting, he was the best qualified by temperament, character ability, sense of loyalty, morals, age, experiences and physique to represent us as the first black player to enter the white majors since the Walker brothers back in the 1880s."

And according to some sources, Irvin actually turned down an offer from the Brooklyn Dodgers' Branch Rickey before Jackie Robinson signed with the team as the first black player of the modern era. Irvin did eventually join the Major Leagues, signing with the New York Giants in 1949.

But before all that, Irvin was a standout high school athlete in New Jersey, catching the attention of baseball and football coaches.

Irvin was born the eighth of 13 children in Haleburg, AL, where his father was a sharecropper. Looking for a better life for their children, his parents moved the family north to Orange, N.J. At Orange High School he was a four-sport star, earning 16 varsity letters.

He was offered a football scholarship from the University of Michigan, but couldn't afford to make the move to Ann Arbor. Instead, he enrolled at Pennsylvania's Lincoln University to play football, but soon left the school when he was offered a contract with the Newark Eagles of the Negro National League.

He played briefly for the team in 1938 as a 19-year-old, then joined the team in 1939. Statistics from the Negro Leagues are incomplete, but Irvin was recognized as one of the great hitters in the league in 1940 and 1941.

After he hit over .400 in 1941, Irvin asked the Eagles for a raise. When the team balked, Irvin opted to sign with Veracruz of the Mexican League. During his sole season in Mexico, Irvin led the league in hitting with a .397 average and a league-leading 20 home runs.

Irvin planned to return to Mexico in 1943, but instead was drafted into the U.S. Army to serve in World War II. He spent the next three years in Europe as part of the 1313th General Services Engineers. He returned stateside after the war ended, but suffered from an inner ear infection as well as other lingering effects from his service.

For the 1946 season, Irvin was again playing for the Eagles. His teammates that year included Larry Doby, who would go on to be the first black player in the American League when he debuted with the Cleveland Indians in 1947. The Eagles won the Negro League World Series that year, beating the Kansas City Monarchs and their star Satchel Paige.

Irvin continued to dominate Negro League pitchers for the next two seasons, before signing with the Giants for $5,000 – a $1,000 pay cut from his Eagles contract. He played in 36 games for the Giants in 1949, hitting .224, but spent most of the year with the Giants' AAA team in Jersey City, where he hit .373.

He spent most of the 1950 season in New York, hitting .299 with 15 home runs and 66 RBI as the Giants finished third in the National League.

Both Irvin and the Giants improved in 1951. Irvin led the league with 121 RBI, with 24 home runs. His .312 average was good for fifth in the league and his .415 on-base percentage was fourth. He also finished in the top 10 in Wins Above Replacement, slugging, runs, hits, total bases, triples, walks and stolen bases. Irvin finished third in voting for the National League MVP behind Roy Campanella and Stan Musial.

The Giants advanced to the World Series that year, winning the National League pennant after they beat the Brooklyn Dodgers in a three-game playoff – made famous by Bobby Thomson's game-winning "Shot Heard 'Round the World" home run. The Giants lost the Series to the New York Yankees in six games. Irvin hit .458 for the Series, tying a World Series record with 11 hits.

Irvin broke his ankle during spring training in 1952, which limited him to 46 games that season. He still hit .310 for the season and was named to his only All-Star Game. His absence may have cost the Giants a repeat pennant, as the team won 92 games, finishing four games behind the Dodgers.

He bounced back in 1953, but the Giants slipped to fifth place as the team lost Willie Mays to military service. Irvin hit .329 with 21 home runs and 97 RBI. His .406 on-base percentage was fourth-best in the National League.

The Giants returned to the World Series in 1954, winning the National League pennant with a 97-57 record. Irvin hit .262 with 19 home runs and 64 RBI for the season. He hit .222 with two RBI in the World Series as the Giants swept the Cleveland Indians in four games.

His ankle injury continued to bother Irvin in 1955 and he played in only 51 games for the Giants before they sent him down to their AAA affiliate, the Minneapolis Millers. In his lone season in Minneapolis, Irvin led the league in hitting with a .352 average as the team won the American Association championship.

Irvin joined the Chicago Cubs for his final Major League season in 1956, hitting .271 with 15 home runs and 50 RBI in 111 games. Irvin played briefly for the Los Angeles Angels of the Pacific Coast League in 1947 before retiring.

After his playing career ended, Irvin worked as a scout and as a public relations specialist for the baseball commissioner's office during Bowie Kuhn's tenure. He also was a representative for the Rheingold beer company.

Irvin was elected to the Mexican Baseball Hall of Fame in 1972 and the National Baseball Hall of Fame in 1973 by a special committee dedicated to the Negro Leagues. The San Francisco Giants retired his No. 20 in 2010.

Irvin died of natural causes in 2016 in Houston at the age of 96.

Jim Kaat

P, Minnesota Twins (1961-73)

Ask Twins fans about Hall of Fame sleights and two names will come to mind: Tony Oliva and Jim Kaat.

Over a 25-year career, Kaat won 283 games – 190 of those with the Washington Senators and Minnesota Twins. He won 16 Gold Gloves, but never a Cy Young or MVP award.

In 2016, Kaat told *Sporting News* he had come to terms with the idea that he may never make the Hall despite some close calls with various Veterans Committees.

"In my own case, I think what works against me is a lot of the voters think it took me too long to accomplish what I accomplished," Kaat said. "If my career ended after the 1975 season, I probably would be in already, because I was a much more dominant pitcher for that 15-year period of time."

Born in Zeeland, MI, in 1938, Kaat was the youngest of four children. In his 2003 biography, *Still Pitching*, Kaat credits his father, John, with nurturing his love of baseball. Although never a player, the senior Kaat was an expert on baseball trivia. Kaat grew up listening to baseball on Detroit and Chicago radio stations.

Kaat played high school baseball and basketball. Although a standout player, he was small in high school, shooting up from 5'10" at graduation to 6'3" by the time he started at nearby Hope College. After his freshman season at Hope, the Washington Senators offered him a tryout at Chicago's Comiskey Park. He impressed them enough to earn an offer of a $4,000 signing bonus, signing with them on June 17, 1957.

Kaat headed to Superior, Neb., to start his minor league career in the Class D Nebraska State League later that year. He finished his first abbreviated pro season with a 5-6 record in 14 games. For 1958, he headed to the Class C Missoula Timberjacks, where he excelled with a 16-9 record, 2.99 ERA, 15 complete games and five shutouts.

Kaat would split the next two seasons between the minor leagues and Washington. When the Senators moved to Minnesota in 1961 and became the Twins, Kaat was in the majors to stay.

The Twins were mediocre in their first season in Minnesota, but Kaat started showing the potential that would make him a mainstay in the Twins rotation for years to come. Kaat finished the year with a 9-17 record and 3.90 ERA in 36 games (29 starts).

But it was 1962 when Kaat (and the Twins) really started to shine. The Twins hung in with the defending World Champion New York Yankees for most of the season, finishing in second place in the American League. Kaat finished 18-14, with a 3.14 ERA, 16 complete games and a league-leading 5 shutouts. He was selected to the All-Star team for the first time and won the first of his 16 straight Gold Glove awards.

Kaat slipped to a 10-10 record with a 4.19 ERA the following season. He bounced back in 1964, but the Twins slipped to sixth place. Kaat still finished the season with a 17-11 record, 3.22 ERA and 13 complete games.

The Twins headed to the World Series in 1965, and Kaat was a key part of the Twins powerhouse rotation, finishing 18-11 with a 2.83 ERA in a league-leading 42 starts. His postseason record was only 1-2 as the Twins lost the World Series that year to the Los Angeles Dodgers, as he had the bad luck to be matched up against the legendary Sandy Koufax in Games 2, 5 and 7. Kaat outpitched Koufax in Game 2, notching a complete game victory, but fell to his pitching brilliance in their final two matchups.

Kaat had his greatest individual season in 1966, with a 25-13 record and 2.75 ERA. He led the league in wins, games started (41), complete games (19) and innings pitched (304 2/3). He was selected for the American League All-Star team and finished fifth in MVP voting. Kaat also won *The Sporting News* Pitcher of the Year Award for the American League. (Koufax won that year's Cy Young award – then given to one pitcher from either league –by unanimous vote.)

Kaat would continue to rack up wins and Gold Glove awards for the Twins for several more seasons. The Twins would return to the playoffs in 1969 and 1970, winning the first two American League West division titles, but falling to the Baltimore Orioles each year.

The Twins slipped in the standings the next few years. In 1973, with the Twins struggling, the team placed Kaat in waivers with the goal of trading him to a contender. It was a move Kaat blamed on Twins owner Calvin Griffith's penny-pinching ways, which he had seen coming since the previous year.

"I was in my midthirties, my salary had crept up to the princely sum of $60,000, and I had battled Calvin Griffith every year at contract time," Kaat wrote in *Still Pitching*. "Because of that, I clearly was not one of Griffith's pets, and I knew he would move me when the opportunity presented itself."

Kaat was claimed by the Chicago White Sox for the $20,000 waiver fee on August 15, 1973.

Kaat left the Twins as one of the most successful pitchers in franchise history, departing with a 190-159 record and 3.34 ERA. His 190 wins as a Senator and Twin are second only to the great Walter Johnson (his 189 wins as a Twin are the most in team history). He's also second to Johnson in innings pitched (3,014 1/3) and games started (433). He pitched in a total of 484 games (No. 4 in franchise history), struck out 1,851 batters (No. 4), threw 133 complete games (No. 5) and completed 23 shutouts (No. 4).

Although he would turn 35 that fall, Kaat's career was far from over. In his first full season with the White Sox, Kaat finished 21-13 with a 2.92 ERA and 15 complete games. He followed that up with his final All-Star season in 1975, pitching his way to a 20-14 record. He finished fourth in voting for the American League Cy Young Award.

Following the 1975 season, the White Sox traded him to the Philadelphia Phillies. Kaat would play seven more seasons for the Phillies, Yankees and St. Louis Cardinals before retiring at the age of 44 after the Cardinals released him in July 1983. Kaat finished his 25-year career with a 283-237 record, 3.45 ERA, 180 complete games, 31 shutouts, 2,461 strikeouts and 4,530 innings pitched over 898 games.

At the time of his retirement, his 25 seasons were the most in Major League history, a mark since surpassed by Nolan Ryan (27 seasons) and Tommy John (26 seasons). He is one of only 29 players to have played in four decades.

In August 1984, Kaat joined the Cincinatti Reds as pitching coach, a role he filled in the 1985 season as well. He started a long broadcasting career in 1986, covering the Yankees and Twins, as well as working on national baseball and Olympics broadcasts. He retired from full-time broadcasting in 2006, but still makes occasional appearances.

In 2001, Kaat was elected to the Twins Hall of Fame and named to the Twins 40th Anniversary All-Time Team. He rejoined the Twins in 2018 as a special assistant.

George "High Pockets" Kelly

1B, Minneapolis Millers (1930-31)

Although the majority of George Kelly's Hall of Fame career was behind him by the time he arrived in Minneapolis in 1930, he was still an important contributor to the team for parts of two seasons.

Born Sept. 10, 1895, in San Francisco, Kelly grew up in the Bay area as a fan of the newly formed Pacific Coast League. He played semipro ball in the area after dropping out of high school and made his professional debut at the age of 18 in 1914 for the Vancouver Bees of the Northwestern League.

He returned to the Bees in 1915 and was impressive enough to catch the eye of the New York Giants, who purchased his contract late that summer. He played in only 17 games that year while hitting only .158. His 1916 season was no better as he again hit .158, this time in 49 games.

In July 1917, having played in only nine games, the Giants placed Kelly on waivers, where he was claimed by the Pittsburgh Pirates. However, the Pirates found little use for him and waived the first baseman in August and the Giants claimed him again. They sent him down to their minor league affiliate, the Rochester Hustlers, where he hit .300 in 32 games.

After spending the 1918 season in military service during World War I, Kelly returned to Rochester in 1919, where he hit .356 with 15 home runs – more than any player except Babe Ruth hit in the majors that year. By the end of the season, he was in New York to stay, where he hit .290 in 32 games.

For the next seven seasons, he was a fixture in the Giants lineup. In 1920, he hit .266 with 11 home runs, while leading the league in 155 games played, 94 RBI and 92 strikeouts.

In 1921, Kelly hit .308 – the first of six straight .300 seasons – with a league-leading 23 home runs and 122 RBI. That year also started a run of success for the Giants as they won the first of four pennants in a row, including World Series titles in 1921 and 1922. Kelly continued to pace the Giants offense during that run, including leading the league in RBI 136 in 1924.

After the 1926 season, the Giants traded Kelly to the Cincinnati Reds for future Hall of Fame outfielder Edd Roush. He posted his final 100 RBI season for the Reds in 1929. He was released by the Reds after 51 games in 1930, despite sporting a .287 average.

It was at that point that he signed on with the Millers. In his 34 games with the team that year, Kelly hit .361 with six home runs. Late in the season, he returned to the National League to play 39 games with the Chicago Cubs.

The Cubs released Kelly in February 1931, and he returned to the Millers for the 1931 season. In his lone full season with the team, he hit .320 with 20 home runs and 112 RBI.

He played briefly for the Brooklyn Dodgers – and the team's minor league affiliate in Jersey City – in 1932. He played in 21 games for the Oakland Oaks of the Pacific Coast League in 1933 before retiring from baseball.

Kelly finished his 16-year Major League career with a .297 average, with 1,778 hits, 148 home runs and 1,020 RBI. He was seen by his peers as a great clutch hitter and standout defender.

After his retirement, Kelly coached with the Reds and Boston Bees. He also worked as a West Coast scout for the Reds and other teams.

Kelly was elected to the Baseball Hall of Fame in 1973 by the Veterans Committee in a controversial vote. The committee at the time included two of his former teammates, Bill Terry and Frankie Frisch, and many baseball historians consider Kelly to fall short of the (albeit subjective) Hall of Fame standard.

Harmon Killebrew

1B/3B/OF, Minnesota Twins (1961-74)

There's little doubt who was the greatest Twin power hitter of all time.

The Killer (as the mild-mannered Killebrew was affectionately known) tops almost every power category in the Twins (and Senators) all-time record book: First in home runs (559), RBI (1,540), walks (1,505), total bases (4,026), Wins Against Replacement (71.2 WAR), slugging percentage (.514), OPS (.892), games played (2,329) and AB per home run (14.0).

Killebrew ranks second in franchise history in at bats and runs scored and sixth in hits.

Killebrew was born June 29, 1936, in Payette, ID, the youngest of four children. His prodigious home run power and athletic skill seems to have come from his father's side of the family. Legend was that his grandfather, Culver Killebrew, was a powerful wrestler and the strongest man in the Union Army. His son, Harmon Sr., or Clay, was born when Culver was nearly 60 years old. Clay went on to play college football, earning All-American honors, and played professionally for the Wheeling (West Virginia) Steelers.

Harmon Jr. excelled at sports at an early age, lettering in baseball, football, basketball and track in high school. He caught the eye of Idaho's U.S. Sen. Herman Welker, who recommended him to the owner of the woeful Washington Senators, Clark Griffith. Griffith sent a scout out to Idaho to take a look at Killebrew. He was impressed enough that the Senators offered Killebrew a contract for $6,000 a year for three years, with a $12,000 signing bonus, a significant sum in 1954.

As a "bonus baby" because of the size of his signing bonus, Killebrew was required to stay on the Senators' major league roster for two seasons. (The rule was in effect from 1947 to 1965 and was designed to limit the richest teams from stockpiling talent in the minor leagues.)

Killebrew made his major league debut on June 23, 1954, as a pinch runner. Not surprisingly, with no minor league experience, Killebrew struggled in those first two seasons. He played in only 47 games between 1954 and 1955, hitting .215 with 4 home runs and 10 RBI, while striking out 34 times.

Once he was eligible to be sent to the minor leagues in 1956, the Senators sent Killebrew to Class A Charlotte. He would spend the next three seasons splitting time between the Charlotte, Chattanooga, Indianapolis and Washington. He put up impressive numbers in the minors, but played little for the Senators.

In 1959, Killebrew finally got a chance at a full-time role in the majors. Senators owner Calvin Griffith – who had taken over the team after Clark's death in 1955 – traded 3B Eddie Yost to make room for Killebrew (and fellow youngster Bob Allison).

Both players rewarded Griffith's faith. The two made the American League All-Star team, while Allison won the AL Rookie of the Year Award. Killebrew hit .242 with a league-leading 42 home runs and 105 RBI, finishing 15th in MVP voting. His 1960 season was shortened by surgery for nasal irritation and a hamstring injury, but he still managed to hit 30 home runs and improve his average to .276.

In 1961, the Senators moved to Minnesota, and Killebrew started a great run of seasons. He hit .288 with a franchise-record 46 home runs and 122 RBI, making his second All-Star team and finishing 11th in MVP voting. It was the beginning of an 11-season run where he be a 10-time All-Star, and receive votes in MVP balloting for all but one season.

He continued to set the pace for American League home run hitters for the next several years, leading the league in 1962 (48), 1963 (45) and 1964 (49). His 126 RBI led the league in 1962 (as did his 142 strikeouts).

The Twins made their first World Series appearance in 1965, but Killebrew missed seven weeks after dislocating his left elbow in a collision at first base. He still managed to slug 25 home runs and return for the World Series, where he would hit .286 with one home run and two RBI as the Twins lost to the Los Angeles Dodgers.

Back to play a full season again in 1966, Killebrew hit .281 with 39 home runs, 110 RBI and a league-leading 103 walks. With the Twins in another pennant race in 1967, Killebrew again led the league with 44 home runs whole finishing second in MVP voting.

Killebrew got off to another solid start in 1968 and was once again named to the All-Star Game. In the game at Houston's Astrodome, Killebrew suffered a hamstring injury and missed most of the rest of the season.

He roared back in 1969, though, to have a career year. He hit .276, and led the league in home runs (49), RBI (140) and walks (145). He was voted the American League MVP as the Twins won the first American League West title. He would be a non-factor in the postseason, hitting .125 with no home runs as the Baltimore Orioles swept the Twins out of the playoffs.

The Twins repeated as division champs in 1970, and Killebrew followed his MVP year with his final 40-home run season. For the season, he hit .271 with 41 home runs and 113 RBI, good enough for a third-0place finish in the MVP race behind Baltimore's Boog Powell and Twins teammate Tony Oliva.

He'd make his final All-Star appearance in 1971, with 28 home runs and a league-leading 119 RBI. On Aug. 10, 1971, Killebrew hit his 500th home run, after waiting 16 games between home runs No. 499 and No. 500.

As the 1972 season started, age and injuries started to catch up to the 36-year-old Killebrew. He still hit 26 home runs, but his average dropped to .231. Sidelined by a knee injury in 1973, Killebrew was limited to only 69 games. He returned in 1974, but hit only 13 home runs with 54 RBI.

Following that 1974 season, the Twins offered Killebrew a contract to be a player-coach or manager for the team's AAA affiliate in Tacoma, WA. But Killebrew wanted to continue playing and after being released on January 16, 1975, by the Twins, he signed with the Kansas City Royals. In his lone season with the Royals, Killebrew hit .199 with 14 home runs and 44 RBI. Early that season, the Twins retired his No. 3, the first retired number in Twins history.

At the time of his retirement, his 573 home runs were the fifth-most in baseball history and the most by an American League right-handed hitter.

Following his retirement as a player, Killebrew returned to Minnesota where he told Griffith he wanted to manage the Twins. Griffith declined, opting for experienced manager Gene Mauch. Killebrew then launched a long career as a broadcaster for the Twins, Oakland Athletics and California Angels.

He was elected to the National Baseball Hall of Fame in his fourth year of eligibility in 1984. In the late 1980s, Killebrew suffered numerous business setbacks, eventually filing for bankruptcy and experiencing health problems.

He eventually moved to Arizona and, in 1998, created the Harmon Killebrew Foundation, dedicated to promoting wellness through sports. He was ranked No. 69 on *The Sporting News* 1998 list of Baseball's 100 Greatest Players of the 20th Century. In 2000, he was a member of the inaugural class of the Twins Hall of Fame. He was named to the Twins 40th Anniversary All-Time Team in 2001.

It was also in the late 1990s that he had a reunion of sorts with the Twins, becoming more involved with the franchise as an ambassador and mentor to future stars including Michael Cuddyer, Torii Hunter, Joe Mauer and Justin Morneau. Among other lessons, he famously taught those players to appreciate the fans and take care with their autographs – a lesson that any fan who has been lucky enough to get their signatures can see they took to heart.

Killebrew was inducted into the World Sports Humanitarian Hall of Fame in 2006. He was also one of four players – along with Rod Carew, Tony Oliva and Kirby Puckett – immortalized in a bronze statue outside the Twins new home at Target Field when it opened in 2010.

He announced in December 2010 that he had been diagnosed with esophageal cancer. He was scheduled to throw out the ball on Opening Day at Target Field in 2011, but his declining health made that impossible. Instead, teammate Tony Oliva did it in his honor. He died at his home on May 17, 2011, at the age of 74. Thousands of fans and teammates turned out for his memorial at Target Field on May 26.

Chuck Knoblauch

2B, Minnesota Twins (1991-97)

These days, Chuck Knoblauch is probably best known for his off-the-field issues, throwing problems – and an unfortunate return to the Metrodome in 2001. But before all that happened, Knoblauch was a key part of the 1991 World Series championship and one of the few reasons to watch the team for the rest of the decade of the '90s.

Born July 7. 1968, in Houston, Knoblauch came from a baseball family. Both his father, Ray, and Uncle Eddie played and managed in the minor leagues. Knoblauch was himself a standout at Bellaire High School, and was drafted by the Philadelphia Phillies in the 18th round of the 1986 draft.

He instead opted to attend Texas A&M University, a move that paid off when the Twins selected him in the first round of the 1989 draft. Knoblauch made his minor-league debut that year with the Class A Kenosha Twins of the Midwest League. In 51 games at Kenosha, Knoblauch hit .286 with a .387 OBP, 13 doubles and nine stolen bases. He finished the season with the Visalia Oaks of the California League, where he hit .364 with a .412 OBP and 21 RBI in only 18 games.

He was less of a success on defense. Drafted as a shortstop, Knoblauch played that position in his first summer in the Twins organization. In just 69 games between his two minor league stops, Knoblauch made 31 errors. For the 1990 season, the Twins moved Knoblauch to 2B, where he would play most of his career.

While learning the new position, Knoblauch made 20 errors, but continued his success at the plate. With the Double A Orlando Sun Rays, he hit .289 with a .389 OBP and 23 doubles, while stealing 23 bases. That was good enough to get him an invite to spring training in 1991, where the cellar-dwelling Twins were once again looking for a second baseman.

Knoblauch impressed enough in Florida that spring to win the starting job, and made his major league debut on April 9, 1991, when the Twins opened their season at the Oakland Athletics. The Twins had finished in last place in the American League West in 1990 with a 74-88 record, 29 games behind Oakland. Although the team still had many players from its 1987 World Series team, there wasn't a lot to indicate the Twins had another run in them.

Even as the 1991 season got going, the Twins struggled. They started out the year with a 2-9 record. On Memorial Day, the Twins were sitting at 20-24, 7 ½ games out of first place. Then on June 1 the Twins beat the Royals in Kansas City – in what ended up being the first of 15 straight wins (and a 22-6 June record) that propelled Minnesota into first place.

The Twins, of course, went on to win the World Series that year, helped greatly by their rookie second baseman. Knoblauch hit .281 on the season, with a .351 OBP, 24 doubles, 50 RBI and 25 stolen bases. That was good enough for Knoblauch to win the American League Rookie of the Year award, capturing 26 of the 28 first-place votes.

He continued his success at the plate in the postseason, hitting .350 in the American League Championship Series against Toronto and .308 (with four stolen bases) against the Atlanta Braves in the World Series. But his greatest contribution to the Twins championship may have come in Game 7 of the Series. In the 8th inning, with the game tied 0-0 and Lonnie Smith on first base, Terry Pendleton drilled a ball into the outfield. Smith lost sight of the ball, and Knoblauch and shortstop Greg Gagne faked a double play. With Smith unsure of where the ball was, he had to slow down while rounding second and ended up having to stop at third. Jack Morris would work his way out of the jam and the rest, as they say, is history. It's worth noting that Smith has since said he knew the ball had gone out of the infield, but either way, it worked out for the Twins.

Knoblauch avoided the sophomore slump in 1992, improving in almost every statistical category. He hit .297 with a .384 OBP and 34 stolen bases, and earned his first All-Star nod. Defensively, Knoblauch made only six errors at 2B and posted a .992 fielding percentage. The Twins dropped to second place that season, but still won 90 games. As it turned out, that would be the Twins final winning season until 2001.

Even as the Twins struggled for the next several seasons, Knoblauch continued to excel at the plate and in the field. Even in 1993, his worst season in a Twins uniform, Knoblauch hit .277 with a .354 OBP, 27 doubles and 29 stolen bases.

His 1994 season was almost one for the record books until the players' strike wiped out the final months of the season. In the strike-shortened season, Knoblauch hit .312 with a .381 OBP, 35 stolen bases and league-leading 45 doubles. Knoblauch had been on pace to break Earl Webb's single-season record of 67 doubles before the players went on strike in August. He also made his second All Star Game that summer.

When the players returned in 1995, Knoblauch picked up where he left off, raising his batting average to .333 for the season. His .424 OBP was among the best in the league and he added 46 stolen bases and 34 doubles, while earning his first Silver Slugger award. Those numbers got even better in 1996, as he had career bests in average (.341), OBP (.448), hits (197), triples (a league-leading 14), home runs (13), RBI (72), walks (98) and total bases (299). Throw in 35 doubles and 45 stolen bases and an All-Star nod for good measure.

While most of his numbers slipped in 1997, Knoblauch still hit .291 with a .390 OBP and a career-high 62 stolen bases, winning his second Silver Slugger award. He also won his only Gold Glove that season and made the All-Star team for the fourth and final time.

After that 1997 season, though, Knoblauch was fed up with Minnesota's losing ways and sought a trade to a contender. In February 1998, the Twins traded him to the New York Yankees for four players,

including Christian Guzman and Eric Milton – who would both make
the American League All Star team in 2001 when the Twins finally
posted another winning season.

During Knoblauch's time in New York, the Yankees won four
American League pennants and three World Series titles. While
Knoblauch had some individual success at the plate, especially in 1998
and 1999, he struggled in the field. After making only 13 errors in
1998, that doubled to 26 in 1999. In 2000, he developed throwing
problems (commonly known as "the yips") and had trouble throwing
the ball to first base. He eventually played most of the stretch run and
the entire postseason that year at designated hitter.

The Yankees moved him to left field in 2001 in an effort to keep his
bat in the lineup. That prompted the infamous "Knoblauch Incident"
during his visit to the Metrodome on May 3. With Knoblauch playing
left field on Dollar Dog Night at the 'Dome, Twins fans began pelting
Knoblauch with a variety of objects including the aforementioned hot
dogs, bottle caps and more. The game was stopped and Twins Manager
Tom Kelly had to venture out to the outfield to try to get fans to stop
their immature behavior – and keep the Twins from having to forfeit
the game.

The moment was rated as No. 47 on the Twins list of 100
Metrodome Moments in 2009. In a 2014 interview with the Minneapolis Star Tribune, Knoblauch reflected on the incident.

> *"It hurt," he said. "I mean, I'm human. I can't even give you any
> details. It was like an out-of-body experience ... that's the part
> of my life that's like, 'Really?' It really meant that much? You're
> trying to hurt me, knowingly throwing a quarter or a marble
> or something at me? It's twisted. It made me bitter about Min-
> nesota, definitely."*

After a final season in Kansas City in 2002, Knoblauch retired at
the age of 33. Since his retirement, he's had a variety of legal issues. He

also admitted he used Human Growth Hormone (HGH) at the end of his career after being named in the Mitchell Report. In 2014, he was elected to the Twins Hall of Fame, but the team cancelled his induction after he was charged with assaulting his ex-wife.

Jerry Koosman

P, Minnesota Twins (1979-81)

J erry Koosman is best known as a member of the 1969 "Miracle Mets" World Championship squad – and for sharing a rookie card with Hall of Famer Nolan Ryan.

But the All-Star pitcher is a native of the state and also spent parts of three seasons with the Minnesota Twins. Koosman was born in 1942 in Appleton, MN., where he grew up working on the family farm. He pitched in in local leagues and American Legion ball, then attended the University of Minnesota-Morris, which didn't have a baseball team.

After being drafted into the U.S. Army in 1962, Koosman eventually ended up at Fort Bliss in El Paso, Texas. He played for the base team, where his catcher was John Luchese, the son of an usher at Shea Stadium, the home of the New York Mets. Word made its way back to New York and in 1964 the Mets signed him with a $1,600 bonus. In an undated interview posted on TwinsTrivia.com, Koosman said he turned down a $10,000 bonus from the Twins.

After spending most of three seasons in the minor leagues, Koosman joined the Mets in 1967. In 1968, he won 19 games, making the first of his two All Star teams for the Mets. He won two games in the World Series for the 1969 team that brought the Mets their first World Championship.

After 12 seasons with the Mets, Koosman was traded by New York to the Twins in December 1978. Koosman made an immediate impact for the Twins, finishing the 1979 season with a 20-13 record for the last Twins team to post a winning record until the 1987 World Series team.

Koosman won 16 games in 1980 as the Twins slipped to a 77-84 record. In 1981, he became the oldest Twins player to throw a complete game when he won 7-0 at Kansas City May 22, at 38 years, 150 days old – a mark since surpassed by Rick Reed in 2003 and 44-year-old Bartolo Colon in 2017. He posted a 3-9 record for the Twins before being traded to the Chicago White Sox shortly after the end of the player's strike that wiped out much of that season. He finished his Twins career with a 39-35 record and 3.77 ERA.

Koosman retired at age 42 after the 1985 season, with a career mark of 222-209, a 3.36 ERA, 140 complete games, 33 shutouts and 2,556 strikeouts. He was inducted into the New York Mets Hall of Fame in 1989.

Joe Mauer

C/1B/DH, Minnesota Twins (2004-18)

On September 30, 2018, Joe Mauer stepped onto the Target Field grass to play catcher. It would be his final appearance as a player and first as a catcher since his career-altering concussion in 2013. He exited the game to a standing ovation from the crowd in the stands and the players on the field. It was the end of the career of a homegrown star, one of Minnesota's own who grew up to live the dream of many local kids.

Mauer was born April 19, 1983, in St. Paul, the youngest of three sons – all of whom would play professional baseball in the Twins organization. From a young age, Mauer was a stand-out athlete. Mauer attended Cretin-Derham Hall High School where he played baseball, basketball and football, excelling at all three sports. He is the only player to be named the *USA Today* High School Player of the Year for two different sports – football in 2000 and baseball in 2001.

He struck out only once in his four-year high school baseball career, and hit .605 during his senior year. As the two-year starting quarterback, he led the school to two state championship games and one state title and was set to play quarterback at Florida State. In basketball, Mauer was an all-state point guard.

The Twins selected Mauer with the No. 1 overall pick in the 2001 draft, a controversial pick at the time as No. 2 pick Mark Prior was considered by most baseball experts to be the superior player. The Twins were accused of picking Mauer instead of Prior in order to save money, while team officials insisted they thought Mauer was the better player. (Prior would end up winning 42 games over five seasons with the Chicago Cubs before recurring arm injuries ended his promising career.)

Mauer would make his pro debut in the summer of 2001, playing 32 games for the Rookie-level Elizabethton Twins. In 110 at-bats, he hit .400, with a .492 on-base percentage.

Mauer played his first full season in 2002 for the Quad Cities River Bandits of the Midwest League. He hit .302, while adding 23 doubles, four home runs and 62 RBI. Mauer had another standout season in 2003, splitting the year between Class A Fort Myers and AA New Britain. In 135 minor-league games, he hit .338 with 30 doubles and 85 RBI. He also played in the Futures Game at that year's All-Star Game in Chicago.

With starting catcher A.J. Pierzynski traded to the San Francisco Giants after the 2003 season, the way was cleared for Mauer to start with the Twins in 2004. He made his major-league debut on April 5, 2004, collecting two hits against the Cleveland Indians.

Just two days later, he suffered a knee injury that would require surgery and cause him to miss more than a month of action. He returned in June, only to be shut down in July with swelling and pain in his knee. He hit .308 in his abbreviated 35-game rookie season. With the injury out of the way, Mauer returned to play his first full season in 2005, hitting .294 with 26 doubles, nine home runs, 55 RBI and 13 stolen bases.

The 2006 season saw the Twins return to the playoffs, with Justin Morneau winning the MVP award and Johan Santana winning the Cy Young as the team made a roaring comeback to capture the division title. Mauer certainly did his part as well, winning his first batting title with a .347 average. That made him the first catcher to win an American League batting title. He added 36 doubles, 13 home runs and 84 RBI, while also earning his first of six All-Star selections and the first of five Silver Slugger awards.

Mauer was again limited by injuries in 2007, playing in only 109 games and racking up a .293 average. He rebounded in 2008 to win his second batting title, hitting .328. He was the starting catcher for the

American League in the All-Star Game, while earning his first of three Gold Gloves in a row and his second Silver Slugger. He finished fourth in voting for the AL MVP award.

The 2009 season would be even better for Mauer, as he posted career highs in several statistical categories. Back pain caused Mauer to miss the first month of season, but he returned May 1 and quickly made up for lost time, hitting a home run on his first swing of the season.

His .365 average, .444 on-base percentage and .587 slugging average all led the league – making him the first American League player to do so since George Brett in 1980. His 191 hits, 28 home runs and 96 RBI were all career highs. That was good enough to win Mauer the AL MVP award that season, while starting in the All-Star Game and winning Gold Glove and Silver Slugger awards. He was also named Player of the year by *Baseball America*.

Shortly before the 2010 season, with the Twins set to move into Target Field, Mauer agreed to an eight-year/$184 million contract extension, the largest in Twins history and biggest ever for a catcher. While Mauer's home run totals dropped in 2010, he did rack up 43 doubles and 75 RBI. His .327 average ranked No. 3 in the league, as did his .402 on-base percentage. He collected his 1,000th career hit in September, while earning another All-Star selection and his third-straight Gold Glove and Silver Slugger awards.

Mauer had knee surgery following the 2010 season and that surgery, along with other ailments, would haunt him throughout the season. In only 82 games, Mauer hit .287 – the lowest mark of his career to that point. Mauer bounced back with two solid seasons in 2012 and 2013, playing in the All-Star Game both seasons with batting averages over .310. His .416 on-base percentage in 2012 led the league, and Mauer earned his fifth Silver Slugger award in 2013.

But in August, the path of Mauer's career would drastically change as he suffered another concussion. After 113 games, Mauer wouldn't return to the field that year. When he did come back in 2014, it would be as a first baseman, and he would never again be the same batter. The differences in Mauer's stats pre- and post-concussion are telling. At the time of his concussion, Mauer had a .323 career batting average, with a .405 on-base percentage and .468 slugging average. After the concussion, he hit .278/.359/.388.

He had his best season post-concussion in 2017, when he hit .305, with 36 doubles and 77 RBI as the Twins earned a Wild Card berth. In 2018, Mauer started his 14th opening day for the Twins, setting a franchise record. He also recorded his 2,000th career hit that season, but missed several games with another concussion.

After the 2018 season, Mauer officially retired from baseball. The Twins retired his No. 7 during the 2019 season.

For his career, Mauer hit .306 with a .388 on-base percentage and .439 slugging average He totaled 2,123 hits, 428 doubles, 143 home runs, 1,018 runs and 923 RBI. His doubles mark and 3,087 times successfully reaching base are both team records, as are his 921 games as a catcher. His hit total is second only to Kirby Puckett in Twins history and he also ranks in the Top 10 in team history in on-base percentage, games played, at bats, RBI and walks.

Willie Mays

OF, Minneapolis Millers (1951)

Willie Mays' time in Minneapolis was brief but quite memorable. The future Hall of Famer and one of the greatest all-around players of all time spent less than two months in 1951 playing at Nicollet Park, but dominated the American Association in his short stint with the Millers.

Minneapolis was the second minor league stop for Mays after he spent the 1950 season with the Trenton Giants. He batted .353 for Trenton, earning him an invitation to spring training with the New York Giants.

Although he impressed the coaches there, the team decided to send him down to Minneapolis to start the season. Even at the time, they didn't expect the stay to be a long one. As Mays writes in his 1988 autobiography:

> As the camp drew to a close, it was obvious I could handle my job. Tommy Heath, the Millers' manager called me into his office one morning and told me, "Willie, we're taking you with us to Minneapolis. But I kind of have the feeling you're not going to spend the whole summer with us. I think it's only a matter of time before the Giants call you up."

His teammates in Minneapolis included two other future Hall of Famers, Ray Dandridge and Hoyt Wilhelm.

The story of his first game with the Millers is now one of legend – and very Minnesotan. Mays – an Alabama native – woke up on opening day to see snow outside. It was only the second time in his life Mays had seen snow. Assuming the team wouldn't play in the snow, he went back to bed. A couple of hours later Heath called to ask where he was.

81

The snow had stopped and they were going to play the game after the team used a helicopter to blow the snow off the field.

Despite showing up late, Mays hit a homer in his debut. It was the beginning of a great run with Minneapolis. In his 35 games with the Millers, Mays batted .477 with eight home runs and 30 RBI.

Helping to ease his transition to AAA baseball were two former Negro League players, Dandridge and Dave Barnhill. He lived across the street from the two players on Minneapolis's Fourth Avenue South, a short walk from the stadium.

He became a fan favorite during his time in Minneapolis, with local enthusiasts realizing they were seeing something special. Thousands of fans turned out to see him play, even across town at the St. Paul Saints stadium.

It didn't take long for his performance to catch the attention of the New York Giants, who called him up to the big leagues on May 24, 1951. When the call came, Mays was reluctant to go, worried he couldn't hit big league pitching. After a profanity-laden response from Giants manager Leo Durocher, Mays was soon on a plane to Philadelphia, where the Giants were playing at the time.

A Milwaukee Brewers official estimated that Mays's departure cost the American Association $250,000 in gate receipts.

The story of Willie Mays starts before Trenton and Minneapolis, of course.

Mays was born May 6, 1931, in Westfield, Alabama. Both his parents – who never married – were talented athletes. His father, Cat Mays, played baseball for the local Negro team. His mother, Annie Satterwhite, was a basketball and track star in high school. Willie was a basketball and football star at Fairfield Industrial High School before graduating in 1950.

His professional baseball career started before he graduated from high school, when he played for the minor league Chattanooga Choo-Choos, a member of the Negro Southern League, during the summer of

1947 at the age of 16. In 1948, he stayed closer to home, playing for the Birmingham Black Barons of the Negro American League. The team advanced to the 1948 Negro League World Series, which it lost 4-1 to the Homestead Grays.

With black players now starting to play in the Major Leagues, several teams started scouting Mays. The Boston Braves were the first to show interest, but were unable to close a deal as the owner of the Black Barons wanted to keep Mays for the rest of the season. Just imagine the possibilities of an outfield that included Mays and Hank Aaron. But the deal was not to be, as the Giants arrived and signed Mays for $4,000 and assigned him to Trenton, where he played before moving up to Minneapolis and New York.

His major league career got off to a bit of a slow start, with Mays hitless in his first 12 at bats. In his 13th at bat, he hit a home run off of future Hall of Famer Warren Spahn of the Braves.

It didn't take long for Mays to show he belonged in New York. He finished the season with a .274 average, 22 doubles, 20 home runs and 68 RBI. He won the National League Rookie of the Year award as the Giants advanced to the World Series. The team lost to the New York Yankees in six games, but Mays made history along with Hank Thompson and Monte Irvin, becoming the first all-African-American outfield in Major League history.

Mays would miss most of the 1952 season and all of the 1953 season when he was drafted into the U.S. Army. He spent most of his time in uniform playing baseball at Fort Eustis, VA. Mays estimated he played 180 games for the Army during his stint.

Mays returned to the Giants in 1954 to lead the team to the World Series. He hit a league-leading .345 with 41 home runs and 110 RBI. He also led the league in slugging (.667) and triples (13). He won his first Most Valuable Player award – the first of 13 straight seasons (and 15 total seasons) that he'd get votes in the MVP race. It was also the first of his 20 consecutive All-Star seasons.

Mays would win the only World Series of his career in 1954, with the Giants sweeping the Cleveland Indians in four games. The Giants wouldn't win another World Series until 2010. That 1954 season also produced one of the iconic moments of Mays's career, "The Catch," an over-the-shoulder running grab by Mays in deep center field of the Polo Grounds of a long drive off the bat of Vic Wertz during the eighth inning of Game 1. The catch prevented two Indian runners from scoring, preserving a tie game.

Mays continued to excel for the Giants. In 1955, he hit .319 with a league-leading 51 home runs. In 1956, he became the first National League player to join the 30-30 club, as he hit 36 home runs and stole a league-leading 40 bases. He followed that up with a second 30-30 season in 1957. He also won the first of 12 straight Gold Gloves that season.

After the 1957 season, the Giants moved to San Francisco. The change in coasts made no difference in Mays's performance. He led the league in stolen bases the first two seasons in San Francisco. In 1960, his 190 hits paced the National League.

In 1962, Mays again led the league in home runs with 49 as he finished second in voting for the MVP award to the Maury Wills of the Los Angeles Dodgers. The Giants would beat the Dodgers in a three-game playoff to return to the World Series for the last time in Mays's career. The Giants lost to the Yankees in seven games.

He'd again lead the league in home runs in 1964, slugging 47 home runs with a league-leading .607 slugging average. Mays won his second MVP award in 1965, hitting .317 with a league-leading and career-high 52 home runs and 112 RBI. His .398 on-base percentage and .645 slugging average also led the league. He hit 37 home runs and had 103 RBI, his final season of 30+ home runs and 100+ RBI, as he finished third in MVP voting.

He hit his 600th career on Sept. 22, 1969, off of Mike Corkins of the San Diego Padres. At the time, only Babe Ruth had reached the 600 home run mark. *The Sporting News* named Mays as the 1960s "Player of the Decade." On July 18, 1970, Mays notched his 3,000[th] hit.

In his final full season with the Giants, Mays in 1971 led the league with 112 walks and a .425 on-base percentage. In May 1972, the Giants traded the 41-year-old Mays to the New York Mets.

Mays homered in his Mets debut May 14, 1972, against his former team. Mays would stay with the Mets through the 1973 season, finishing his career in the 1973 World Series as the Mets lost to the Oakland Athletics in seven games. At 42, he was the oldest position player to appear in a World Series game.

He retired with a .302 average, 3,283 hits, 660 home runs, 523 doubles, 2,062 runs, 140 triples, 1,903 RBI and 338 stolen bases. His lifetime total of 7,095 outfield putouts is a major league record. His 24 All-Star game appearances are tied with Hank Aaron and Stan Musial for the most in baseball history.

Mays was elected to the Hall of Fame in 1979 in his first year of eligibility. His No. 24 has been retired by the Giants. In 1999, Mays was ranked No. 2 on the Sporting News's list of the 100 Greatest Baseball Players and named to the Major League Baseball All-Century Team. President Barack Obama presented him with the Presidential Medal of Freedom in 2015.

Paul Molitor

DH/3B/2B/1B
University of Minnesota Golden Gophers (1974-77)
Minnesota Twins (1996-98); Manager (2014-18)

A St. Paul native, Paul Molitor returned to the North Star State to finish his Hall of Fame career.

Born Aug. 22, 1956, in St. Paul, he was the fifth of eight children. He grew up a fan of the Twins, especially outfielder Bob Allison (with whom he would end up sharing his uniform No. 4).

As a child and teenager, he played on the same Oxford neighborhood playground where another future Hall of Famer, Dave Winfield, had recently played. He also occasionally played against Jack Morris – another St. Paul native and Hall of Famer. He attended Cretin High School (now Cretin-Derham Hall) where other alumni include future Twins catcher Joe Mauer.

He was all-state in both baseball and basketball and was selected in the 28th round of the 1974 draft by the St. Louis Cardinals. Molitor instead opted to attend the University of Minnesota on a baseball scholarship, where he played for legendary coach Dick Siebert. Following three standout seasons at Minnesota, Molitor was drafted third overall in the 1977 draft by the Milwaukee Brewers.

He made the major league club for opening day of 1978 after only half a season at Class A Burlington, IA. With incumbent shortstop Robin Yount injured, Molitor was named the opening day starting shortstop and leadoff hitter. Molitor moved to second base when Yount returned. He finished the season with a .273 average and 30 stolen bases, good enough for him to finish second in voting for the American League Rookie of the Year award.

Molitor continued to improve in 1979, hitting .322, the first of 12 career .300 seasons. He made his first All-Star team in 1980, but didn't play in the game after he pulled a muscle in his rib cage. It was the beginning of a run of injuries that would hamper Moltor during his Brewers career.

After an ill-fated move to the outfield and another injury led to a subpar 1981 season, Molitor returned to the infield in 1982. Playing third base, he had a league-leading 666 at bats and rebounded to hit .302 with 201 hits, 41 stolen bases and 136 runs. The Brewers also made their only World Series appearance to date, beating the California Angels in the ALCS as Molitor hit .316 and slugged .684. Although Molitor would hit .355 in the World Series, the Brewers lost to the St. Louis Cardinals in seven games.

Molitor would play 10 more seasons in Milwaukee, earning four more All-Star nods and winning the Silver Slugger award in 1987 and 1988. In 1987, Molitor had a 39-game hitting streak, the fifth-longest in modern-day baseball history. For the season, he hit .353, with a league-leading 41 doubles and 114 runs, but was limited to 118 games as the injury issues continued.

After the 1992 season, Molitor signed a free agent contract with the defending World Champion Toronto Blue Jays. He made an immediate impact for the Blue Jays, making his sixth All-Star team, winning his third Silver Slugger award and finished second to Frank Thomas in voting for the MVP award. He hit .332, with 111 RBI, 121 runs and a league-leading 211 hits.

He helped the Blue Jays advance to the World Series again, as they beat the Chicago White Sox in the ALCS, with Molitor hitting .391 with an OPS of 1.177. He topped that in the World Series as the Blue Jays bested the Philadelphia Phillies in six games. Molitor was voted the World Series MVP as he hit .500 with two home runs and eight RBI.

Molitor hit .341 in the strike-shortened 1994 season as he played in a league-leading 115 games. He played one more season in Toronto before signing with his hometown Twins in December 1995.

Despite being one of the oldest players in baseball, the 40-year-old Molitor played in 161 games in 1996. He had a league-leading and career-high 225 hits, with 41 doubles and a career-high 113 RBI, while his .341 average was good for third in the American League. He captured his fourth Silver Slugger award. On September 16, he notched his 3,000th hit in a game against the Kansas City Royals.

He played two more successful seasons in Minnesota despite some injuries. On August 8, 1998, he collected his 500th career stolen base a few weeks before turning 42. He retired after the 1998 season, finishing his career with a .306 average, an .817 OPS, 3,319 hits, 605 doubles, 1,782 runs, 1,307 RBI and 504 stolen bases. His .312 average as a Twin ranks him fourth in team history.

He is one of only five players in major league history with a .300 career average, 3,000 hits and 500 stolen bases, joining Ty Cobb, Honus Wagner, Eddie Collins and Ichiro Suzuki.

The Sporting News ranked him No. 99 on its list of Baseball's 100 Greatest Players in 1998. The Brewers retired Molitor's No. 4 in 1999 and in 2004 he was elected to the Hall of Fame in his first year of eligibility.

After retiring, Molitor stayed with the Twins as the team's bench coach for three seasons and was considered one of the leading candidates to replace Tom Kelly as manager when Kelly retired following the 2001 season. Molitor left the Twins after Ron Gardenhire was hired as the team's manager, but returned to the organization in 2005 to serve as a roving minor league instructor.

He was named to the Twins All-Metrodome Team in 2009.

In 2014, Molitor rejoined the major league club as a coach and was named the Twins manager when Gardenhire was fired following the 2014 season. In 2017, he was named AL Manager of the Year after leading the Twins to their first playoff berth since 2010, following a 103-loss 2016 season. The Twins fired Molitor as manager after the team missed the playoffs in 2018.

Justin Morneau

1B, Minnesota Twins (2003-13)

It's one of the great "What ifs" of Twins history. What if Justin Morneau had slid a little differently when trying to break up that double play? What if John McDonald's knee had just been a little to the right or left? Who is to say how Twins history might have played out if July 7, 2010, hadn't happened?

But that wasn't to be, as Morneau suffered a concussion that caused him to miss the rest of that 2010 season and endure lingering symptoms for the rest of his career. Morneau was in the middle of a career year that season. Through 81 games, he was batting a career-high .345 with a league-leading .437 on base percentage, a .618 slugging average, 18 home runs and 25 doubles. Perhaps not coincidentally, 2010 was also the Twins last division title to date, ending their great run during the 2000s.

Morneau was born May 15, 1981, in New Westminster, British Columbia. Growing up, Morneau played basketball, hockey and baseball, emerging as a star in all three sports.

In high school he was a member of Canadian national champion baseball teams in 1997 and 1998. He also played for the Portland Winter Hawks of the Western Hockey League in 1998, serving as the third-string goalie and playing in one preseason game. Morneau graduated from New Westminster Secondary School in 1999 and was selected (as a catcher) by the Twins in the third round of the 1999 draft.

Morneau made his brief professional debut later that year, playing 17 games for the GCL Twins, hitting .302 for the rookie-level team. Morneau split the 2000 season between the GCL Twins and Elizabethton Twins as the franchise moved him from catcher to first base. He continued to excel at the plate, hitting .382 with 11 home runs and 61 RBI in 58 games.

Morneau continued to work his way up the ranks of the minor leagues in 2001, 2002 and 2003. In 2002, Morneau played for the World Team in the All-Star Futures Games. On June 10, 2003, Morneau made his major league debut against the Colorado Rockies. In 40 games with the Twins that season, he hit .226 with four home runs, although he spent most of the season with the AAA Rochester Red Wings.

He returned to Rochester to start the 2004 season, but rejoined the Twins for good when the team traded starting first baseman Doug Mientkiewicz to the Boston Red Sox. In 74 games, he hit .271 with a .340 on-base percentage and 19 home runs as the Twins won their third straight division title.

The 2005 season wasn't as productive for Morneau or the Twins even as he played most of the season. In April 2005, he was hit in the head by a pitch and, in a precursor of his future issues, seemed to suffer from the lingering effects most of the season. He finished the year with a .239 average, but did manage to hit 22 home runs.

Morneau and the Twins rebounded in a big way in 2006. He hit .321 with a .375 on-base percentage, .559 slugging average 34 home runs, 130 RBI and 37 doubles – all career highs. He won his first silver slugger award and the American League MVP award as the Twins won the AL Central on the final day of the season. The Twins were swept by Oakland in the Divisional Series, but Morneau hit .417 with two home runs in three games.

The Twins missed the playoffs in both 2007 and 2008, but Morneau continued to post solid numbers for the club. In 2007, he hit 31 home runs, making him the first Twins player since Gary Gaetti to post back-to-back 30 home run seasons. He was named to his first All Star Game and played in that year's Home Run Derby.

Before the 2008 season, Morneau signed a six year/$80 million contract that was the largest in Twins history up to that time. He played in every game that year, hitting .300 with 23 home runs and 129

RBI. He played in his second All-Star Game and won that year's Home Run Derby. Morneau also won his second Silver Slugger award, while finishing second in AL MVP voting to Boston's Dustin Pedroia. He also won the Lionel Conacher Award as the Canadian Male Athlete of the Year.

In 2009, Morneau was named to the Twins All-Metrodome team in the final season at the stadium. That year, Morneau hit 30 home runs with 100 RBI – the last time he would hit either of those marks. He played in his final All-Star Game that summer before suffering a stress fracture in his back that caused him to miss the end of the season and the playoffs. Morneau was voted as a starter in the 2010 All-Star Game, but missed the game after his concussion.

Morneau returned to the Twins after his concussion, but never seemed to be the same player. In 69 games in 2011, he hit .227 with four home runs. His numbers improved in 2012, hitting .267 with 19 home runs in 134 games. He played in 127 games for the Twins in 2013, slugging 17 home runs with a .259 average. On August 31, the Twins traded Morneau to the Pittsburgh Pirates for Alex Presley and a player to be named later.

Morneau finished his Twins career with a .278 average, 860 RBI, 289 doubles and a .347 on-base percentage. His 221 home runs rank behind only Harmon Killebrew and Kent Hrbek as a Twin and his .485 slugging percentage is the second-highest in Twins history.

After finishing the 2013 season with the Pirates, Morneau signed a two-year contract with the Colorado Rockies. In his first season with the Rockies, Morneau showed some of his old form, winning the National League batting title with a .319 average, adding 17 home runs, 32 doubles and 82 RBI.

In May 2015, Morneau suffered another concussion while diving for a ball against the Los Angeles Angels. It would hinder him for the rest of the season as he played in only 49 games. In June 2016, Morneau signed with the Chicago White Sox. He played in 58 games for the Sox that year, hitting .261 with six home runs.

Morneau played for the Canadian team in the 2017 Baseball Classic, but didn't sign with a team during the season. In January 2018, Morneau officially announced his retirement and joined the Twins as a special assistant.

Jack Morris

Pitcher
Minnesota Twins (1991)
St. Paul Saints (1996)

Jack Morris may have only spent one season with the Minnesota Twins, but what a memorable season it was.

Morris was born in St. Paul on May 16, 1955. He attended Highland Park High School in St. Paul, graduating in 1973. He played college ball for Brigham Young University before he was selected by the Detroit Tigers in the fifth round of the 1976 draft.

In 14 years with the Tigers, Morris established himself as one of the best pitchers and ultimate competitors in the American League. He was a four-time All Star with the Tigers and was recognized as Pitcher of the Year in 1981 by *The Sporting News*. In 1984, he helped the Tigers make their way to the World Series, winning 19 games. He went 3-0 in three starts in the postseason, winning the Babe Ruth Award for the best postseason performance, as the Tigers won the World Series.

Morris tried to sign with the Twins following the 1986 season, but that was during the period when the owners colluded not to sign free agents from other teams in an attempt to keep salaries down. Morris has said in multiple interviews that the Twins were his first choice that offseason, but that General Manager Andy MacPhail made it clear the Twins weren't going to sign him.

The Tigers headed to the postseason again in 1987. Luckily for Twins fans, though, Morris gave up 6 runs over 8 innings in losing his lone start for the Tigers in the American League Championship Series.

The St. Paul native was awarded free agency in 1990 as a result of the collusion scandal and finally signed with the Twins, joining the club for the 1991 season. He was an important stabilizing force for the pitching rotation, joining young hurlers Scott Erickson and Kevin Tapani. Morris finished the regular season with an 18-12 record and

3.43 ERA, while appearing in his fifth All Star Game and finishing fourth in voting for the American League Cy Young Award.

> *"The guy was the ultimate competitor," Tapani told* Sports Illustrated *in 2003. "If we were running wind sprints, he'd try to beat you. Scott Erickson and I would take turns running hard. That way we'd save energy so one of us would always be strong enough to beat him. But Jack would run all 16 sprints hard and beat us every time. He had this attitude, 'Whatever you do, I'm going to beat you.'"*

He won both of his starts against the Toronto Blue Jays in the American League Championship Series. But where Morris etched his name in Twins history was with his World Series performance. He started three games, finishing 2-0 with a 1.17 ERA. His 10-inning shutout performance in Game 7 is considered one of the greatest games in World Series history. In 2011, the MLB Network ranked the 1-0 game as the second-greatest in the last 50 years.

Twins manager Tom Kelly was determined to let his ace continue to pitch as long as he could. Morris has said he would have gone out for an 11th inning if necessary.

> *"He put his ass on the line by leaving me in there, and you don't realize it at the time," Morris told the* St. Paul Pioneer Press *in 2011 while watching the game with Kelly. "You start reflecting back about the reality of the situation, and even me, if I was managing, I'd say to myself, 'Man, I've got Rick Aguilera, who's done a pretty damn good job. What do you do here?' And he did something that 99 percent of the baseball world wouldn't do, and without him doing it, I wouldn't be sitting here today."*

Morris won the 1991 World Series MVP Award and his second Babe Ruth Award.

For Morris, that 1991 season would be his lone one with the Twins, as he signed as a free agent with the Blue Jays that winter. His 1992 season was another good one as he went 21-6, leading the league in wins for the eventual World Series champion. He struggled in 1993, finishing 7-12 with a 6.19 ERA. In 1994 he signed with the Cleveland Indians, winning 10 games before being released in August of the strike-shortened season. After failing to make the Cincinnati Reds club after the 1995 spring training, Morris announced his retirement.

Morris wasn't quite done with Minnesota baseball, though. In 1996, he joined the St. Paul Saints of the independent Northern League in a comeback attempt.

"It's pretty basic for me: I want to get on the mound," Morris told Neal Karlen for his 1999 book, *Slouching Toward Fargo*. "I love pitching and it's eating away at me. I want to go out pitching the way I want to go out pitching."

He went 5-1 with a 2.69 ERA in 10 starts. The New York Yankees offered him a contract, but wanted Morris to start with the AAA Columbus Clippers. Morris balked and turned down the offer rather than head to Ohio. With no other offers coming from the major leagues, Morris retired for good after the Saints won the first-half title.

"I was respectful and understanding of his wishes," former St. Paul Saints Manager Marty Scott told the *St. Paul Pioneer Press* in 2014. "Jack said, 'No clubs are calling. I proved to myself I could still pitch. I'm going to retire.' And he did."

Morris finished his career with a 254-186 record, including 162 wins in the 1980s – the most that decade. He pitched 175 complete games over his 18-year career and struck out 2,478 batters.

Since his retirement, Morris has worked as a part-time television analyst for the Blue Jays, Tigers and Twins.

After failing in 15 attempts to be voted in by the Baseball Writers Association of America, Morris was finally elected to the Baseball Hall of Fame in 2017 by the Veterans Committee, along with former Tigers teammate Alan Trammell. Morris's No. 47 was retired by the Tigers in 2018.

Joe Nathan

P, Minnesota Twins (2004-11)

O n Sept. 3, 2017, Joe Nathan ended his 16-year career by signing a one-day contract with the Twins and announcing his retirement. It brought him full-circle to the team where he enjoyed his greatest success, racking up 260 saves on the Twins division title teams of the 2000s.

Nathan was born Nov. 22, 1974, in Houston before his family moved to New York, where he attended Pine Bush High School. At Pine Bush, Nathan played baseball and basketball, while also running track. With no interest from larger schools, Nathan played baseball for Division III Stony Brook University, mostly as a shortstop.

The San Francisco Giants selected Nathan in the sixth round of the 1995 draft. The 20-year-old shortstop played in 56 games at Class A Bellingham that year, hitting .232. When the Giants asked him to convert to pitcher, Nathan opted to return to Stony Brook to finish his education.

After graduation, though, Nathan decided to give pitching a try, returning to the Giants. He spent the 1997 season pitching for the Salem-Keizer Volcanoes. He split his time between the bullpen and the rotation, pitching in 18 games, recording two saves and making five starts while posting a 2.47 ERA.

Nathan spent the 1998 season as a full-time starter in Class A and Class AA. He made his major league debut on April 21, 1999, pitching seven shutout innings and getting his first major league win. For the rest of the 1999 season, he bounced back and forth between the majors and the minors, finishing his big-league season with a 7-4 record and 4.18 ERA in 19 games (14 starts), while also earning his first save.

He continued to spend time in the majors and minors in 2000, struggling with injury as he split time between the bullpen and rotation. After surgery that fall, he spent all of 2001 and most of 2002 in the minors, returning to the Giants to pitch in four games at the end of the 2002 season.

The 2003 season ended up being Nathan's breakout year with the Giants, as he spent the entire season pitching out of the bullpen. In 78 games, Nathan posted a 12-4 record with a 2.96 ERA, while striking out 83 in only 79 innings. That November the Giants sent Nathan, along with fellow pitchers Francisco Liriano and Boof Bonser, to the Twins for catcher A.J. Pierzynski.

Despite the fact that Nathan had only one career save to that point, the Twins made him their closer in 2004. It proved to be a prescient move, as Nathan saved 44 games (blowing only three opportunities) while posting a 1.62 ERA for the AL Central Champion Twins. He made his first All-Star appearance, while finishing fourth in voting for the American League Cy Young Award and receiving votes for AL MVP as well.

Nathan followed that up in 2005 with another All-Star appearance, racking up 44 saves. In 2006, he again received votes for the Cy Young and MVP awards as he recorded 36 saves with a 7-0 record and 1.58 ERA.

From 2007 to 2009, Nathan would save 123 games with only 15 blown saves. He was selected to the American League All-Star team in 2008 and 2009, and shared the 2009 AL Rolaids Relief Man award with the New York Yankees' Mariano Rivera. His 47 saves in 2009 are a team record. He was also named to the Twins' All-Metrodome team in 2009. He would struggle in the postseason, though, blowing his only save opportunity.

During spring training in 2010, Nathan tore his ulnar collateral ligament and opted for Tommy John surgery, causing him to miss the entire 2010 season. He returned to the Twins in 2011, but would struggle for much of the season as he worked his way back from the surgery. He pitched in 48 games, posting a career-high 4.84 ERA, and recording 14 saves. He did become the Twins all-time saves leader that season, picking up his 255th save on Aug. 10, 2011, passing Rick Aguilera.

Overall, he finished his Twins career with 260 saves and a 2.16 ERA in 460 games (fourth in Twins history). His 394 games finished are second only to Aguilera in franchise history.

The Twins opted not to pick up his option after the season, and Nathan signed with the Texas Rangers on Nov. 21, 2011. Nathan would be an All-Star in both of his two seasons with the Rangers. On April 12, 2013, Nathan saved the 300th game of his career against the Tampa Bay Rays.

Nathan signed with the Detroit Tigers before the 2014 season. After a successful 2014 season, Nathan would again require Tommy John surgery early in the 2015 season. He would return to pitch in 2016, making a handful of appearances with the Chicago Cubs and San Francisco Giants that year.

Nathan was invited to spring training with the Washington Nationals in 2017. While he did pitch for the team's AAA affiliate in Syracuse that year, the Nationals released him on May 31. He then signed the one-day contract with the Twins to finish out his career.

All told, Nathan finished his career with 377 saves, eighth-most in Major League history at the time of his retirement. Nathan's 374 American League saves are second only to Rivera, while his 89.33 save percentage is the most for any pitcher with more than 200 career saves.

Joe Niekro

P, Minnesota Twins (1987-88)

Joe Niekro pitched in only 24 games over parts of two seasons for Minnesota. He posted a 5-10 record with a 6.67 ERA in his time as a Twin.

But the events of August 3, 1987, would guarantee he would be remembered as part of Twins lore. That was the night that Niekro, in a game against the California Angels in Anaheim, was ejected after umpire Tim Tschida suspected the knuckleballer of doctoring the ball. When the umpires asked him to empty his pockets, an emery board flew out of his pocket.

After the game, Niekro said he always carried an emery board during games because as a knuckleball pitcher, "I sometimes have to file my nails between innings."

American League President Bobby Brown didn't buy the explanation and suspended the pitcher for 10 games. Later that year Niekro appeared on *Late Night with David Letterman* to poke fun at the incident, complete with a workman's utility belt with a sander, emery boards, Vaseline and more.

During the 1987 season, Joe and his older brother, 300-game-winner and future Hall of Famer Phil Niekro, wrote regular letters to each other, chronicling the season. Those letters were compiled in *The Niekro Files*, a 1988 book.

Joe writes about the emery board incident, in a letter dated August 4:

> *I was attacked on the mound, big brother. That's the simplest way for me to describe it. It was premeditated. I received no warning. I was shown no evidence of scuffed baseballs. ...*

The bottom line, big brother, is those four umpires accused a Niekro of cheating. They've put a black mark on the Niekro name, which is a shame and an insult to hard-working, God-fearing people like Mom and Dad. Momma raised no cheaters.

While the August 1987 suspension may be what Niekro is best known for these days, he was plenty successful as a pitcher before coming to the Twins.

Joe Niekro was born Nov. 7, 1944, in Martins Ferry, Ohio. The Niekros' father (also Phil Niekro) was a coal miner who learned to throw a knuckleball from another miner. He then taught his sons the pitch in their backyard.

Both brothers played baseball for Bridgeport High School. The school's baseball field was renamed "The Niekro Diamond" in 2008 after the brothers. Joe also played college ball at West Liberty University in West Liberty, Virginia. He was drafted by the Cleveland Indians in the January 1966 draft, but didn't sign with the club. When he was picked by the Chicago Cubs in the June draft later that year, he immediately signed with the team.

That year, he pitched in 17 games across three minor league teams. He made his major league debut with the Cubs in 1967, posting a 10-7 record with a 3.34 ERA. He won 14 games in 1968 and was traded to the San Diego Padres after four games in April 1969. He moved on to the Detroit Tigers and the Atlanta Braves, where he and Phil were teammates in 1973 and 1974.

The Houston Astros purchased Joe's contract from the Braves in April 1975 for $35,000. On May 29, 1976, Joe hit the only home run of his career – off of brother Phil.

In Houston, Niekro perfected his knuckleball and had the most success of his career. His 144 wins in an Astros uniform are still a franchise record.

In 1979, he won 21 games, tying brother Phil for the league lead in wins and hurling a league-leading 5 shutouts. He made his sole All-Star Game appearance, finished second in Cy Young voting to the Cubs' Bruce Sutter and sixth in balloting for the National League Most Valuable Player award.

He posted a 20-12 record in 1980, finishing fourth in voting for the Cy Young award. That same year, the Astros tied the Los Angeles Dodgers for the National League West title. In a one-game playoff, Niekro pitched a complete game to lead the Astros to a 7-1 win.

The Astros advanced to the National League Championship Series where they would lose to the Philadelphia Phillies in five games. Niekro pitched 10 shutout innings in his Game 3 start, getting a no-decision, although the Astros won in 11 innings.

In the strike-shortened 1981 season, Niekro went 9-9 with a 2.82 ERA. In that season's split-season playoff format, the Astros won the second-half National League West title. They played the Dodgers in the first round of the playoffs, losing in five games to the eventual World Series winners. In his lone start, Niekro pitched 8 shutout innings in the Astros 11-inning Game 2 win.

He'd reach double digits in wins in each of the next four seasons, but the Astros wouldn't return to the playoffs for the rest of Niekro's tenure. In September 1985, the Astros traded Niekro to the New York Yankees. He and Phil would briefly be teammates again, with the Yankees releasing Phil before the 1986 season.

Niekro spent the 1986 season and the beginning of the 1987 season with the Yankees before they traded him to the Twins on June 7, 1987. While Niekro initially pondered retiring rather than reporting to the Twins, he quickly felt welcome in his new home, as related in his June 10 letter in *The Niekro Files*:

> *I woke up this morning, after pitching my first game for the Twins last night, and I actually felt relaxed, happy, at peace. I*

feel like a boulder the size of a pickup truck has been lifted off
my shoulders. ...

It's a situation with the Twins where you can't wait to get to the
ballpark. I'm having trouble remembering when I last felt that
way.

The 42-year-old Niekro won his first two starts for the Twins before injuring his shoulder during a bench-clearing brawl against the Brewers in Milwaukee. Niekro returned to pitch again after missing a couple of starts, but struggled the rest of the season, even as the Twins won their first World Series that fall. On Sept. 28, he started the Twins win against the Texas Rangers that clinched the division title.

Niekro didn't pitch in the Twins' American League Championship Series against the Detroit Tigers, but did throw two shutout innings in the Twins Game 4 loss in St. Louis. It was Niekro's only World Series appearance in his long career.

He returned to the Twins in 1988, but was released in May after posting a 1-1 record with a 10.03 ERA in five games. He finished his career with a 221-204 record, with a 3.59 ERA. His 221 wins are 77th in baseball history as of the 2018 season.

The 539 games won by the Niekro brothers is the most won by any brother duo in major league history. Niekro was inducted into the National Polish-American Sports Hall of Fame in 1992.

When Phil managed the Colorado Silver Bullets woman's professional baseball team in the 1990s, Joe served as the pitching coach.

His son, Lance, played for the San Francisco Giants as a first baseman from 2003 to 2007. In 2009, he attempted to make a comeback as a knuckleball pitcher and pitched one season in the Atlanta Braves system.

Niekro died October 27, 2006, in Tampa, Florida, after suffering a brain aneurysm. After his death, daughter Natalie founded The Joe

Niekro Foundation to support research, treatment and awareness of brain aneurysms, arteriovenous malformation and hemorrhagic strokes.

Tony Oliva

OF/DH, Minnesota Twins (1962-76)

He's one of the greatest hitters in Minnesota Twins history, but recurring injuries shortened his career and derailed Tony O's Hall of Fame trajectory.

In an era strongly dominated by pitching, Oliva put up strong offensive numbers and was one of the most feared hitters in the American League in his prime. He's among the Twins all-time leaders in batting average, hits, wins against replacement, total bases, doubles, home runs and RBI.

Born July 20, 1938, in Pinar del Rio, Cuba, Pedro Oliva Jr. was the third of 10 children. He learned the game of baseball from his father Pedro, who was a talented player in his own right. Playing from a young age, he honed his skills against local competition in the baseball-rich country.

He signed with the Twins in February 1961 as, it turned out, one of the last Cuban players to make their way to the United States. As relations worsened between Fidel Castro's Cuba and the United States, the once robust stream of baseball players dried out.

There are several versions of what exactly happened next with Oliva, but the end result was that he used the birth certificate of his younger brother, Antonio, to get the passport he needed to make his way to the U.S. With that identification in hand, Pedro became Tony, the name he would be known by throughout his career. It also led to the confusion around his birth date which is variously listed as 1938, 1940 or 1941, depending on the source. Oliva himself has shared various versions of the information over the years.

After further immigration-related delays, Oliva did arrive in Florida for the end of spring training, but was only able to play in a handful games. Although he hit well, his rough play in the field failed to impress the Twins.

Further exacerbating the problem was that of Minnesota's lower-level minor league affiliates, only the Erie, PA, club was able to accept black-skinned players. And that club had recently filled its final roster spot. It appeared the career of the future Twin great might end before it ever got started.

Joe Cambria, the scout who had signed Oliva, intervened on behalf of the young Cuban and two of his countrymen. He lobbied Phil Howser, the general manager of the Twins' Class A team in Charlotte, NC, for help in finding spots for the players. After several weeks, Howser was able to place Oliva with the Class D club in Wytheville, VA, of the Appalachian League.

Oliva struggled with language and cultural differences and also had to adapt to a segregated community. At the same time, his defensive struggles continued as he played night games under lights for the first time.

However, he impressed with his bat as he dominated the league's young pitchers. In only 64 games, he hit .410, hit 10 home runs and knocked in 81 runs. That performance was good enough to get him moved up to Class A Charlotte in 1962. His success continued there, as he hit .350 with 17 home runs, 35 doubles and 93 RBI.

He was promoted to Minnesota at the end of the season, hitting .444 in nine games. The Twins invited Oliva to spring training in 1963, but assigned him to AAA Dallas-Fort Worth of the Pacific Coast League despite a strong performance. At Dallas, Oliva got off to a slow start, but finished the season with a .304 average, 23 home runs, 30 doubles and 74 RBI. He'd once again get a brief cup of coffee with the Twins that fall, hitting .429 in seven at-bats.

By 1964, the Twins had seen enough and were ready to make Oliva a full-time member of the big league club. It was a decision that immediately paid off for Minnesota and Oliva.

That 1964 season is one of the great rookie campaigns. His 217 hits – best in the major leagues – were the third-most recorded by a rookie up to that point. His 374 total bases – also best in baseball – tied the rookie record set by Hal Trotsky in 1934. Oliva also led the league in hitting (.323), runs (109) and doubles (43). He added 32 home runs and 94 RBI. His .557 slugging average was third behind only Boog Powell and Mickey Mantle.

Oliva's fellow players voted him into that year's All-Star Game – his first of eight straight nods for the midsummer classic. He was a near unanimous pick for the American League Rookie of the Year award and finished fourth in voting for MVP. Even more impressive was the fact that Oliva suffered hand and shoulder injuries early in his rookie season. The hand injury would eventually require surgery following the 1965 season.

But first was that magical 1965 season when the Twins brought the American League pennant to Minnesota. Oliva continued his assault on American League pitchers that year, winning another batting title with a .321 average, making him the first player to win batting titles in his first two seasons. He also slugged 16 home runs, stole 19 bases, hit 40 doubles and knocked in 98 runs. He led the league in hits with 185, and finished among the league leaders in several other categories.

Oliva was named American League Player of the Year by *The Sporting News*, made another All-Star appearance that year and finished second to teammate Zoilo Versalles in MVP balloting.

In what would turn out to be the only World Series appearance during his playing career, Oliva struggled as the Twins lost to the Los Angeles Dodgers. He managed only a .192 average with one home run during the seven-game series.

Following his offseason surgery, Oliva returned to the field with another successful season in 1966, even as the Twins fell to second place, nine games behind the pennant-winning Orioles. His .307 average was good for second in the league behind Frank Robinson, while his 191 hits paced the American League. He also won his only Gold Glove award that year.

Oliva continued to be a reliable contributor to the Twins lineup for the next several seasons even as his hereditary knee issues began to take their toll. All told, he would end up having eight knee surgeries during his playing days, along with other assorted injuries. In 1968, he missed more than 30 games, the first time he had to miss a significant chunk of playing time.

Despite that, Oliva was still a key member of the Twins 1969 and 1970 division-winning teams. In 1969, he hit .301, with 24 home runs and 101 RBI, while leading the league with 197 hits and 39 doubles. He had another strong season in 1970, with a .325 batting average, 23 home runs and 107 RBI. He again led the junior circuit in hits (204) and doubles (36). That 1970 season would end up being Oliva's last to not be significantly affected by his injuries.

As the 1971 season started, Oliva was playing the best baseball of his career. On June 29, Oliva was leading the league in hitting with a .375 average and home runs with 18 as the Twins played the Oakland Athletics in Oakland. Diving for a ball hit by A's outfielder Joe Rudi, Oliva slipped and fell hard on his right knee. Oliva would return to the lineup after only a few days, but he would miss time on-and-off during the season. He still ended up leading the league in hitting with a .337 average for his third and final batting title.

On Sept. 22, 1971, Oliva had surgery to remove torn cartilage from the injured knee. He was expected to return in 1972, but by spring training it was clear the knee was still not right. He continued to have swelling and fluid build up on the knee. Running was near impossible and Oliva was unable to play defense. His 1972 season finally ended in June after Oliva was able to play in only 10 games. He had another surgery in July of that year.

Even after that 1972 surgery, Oliva had trouble running, so playing defense was going to be challenging if not impossible for the Twins star. Luckily, the American League owners, in an attempt to boost offense, voted to add the designated hitter in 1973. It was in that role that Oliva would play his final four seasons in a Twins uniform. While not the offensive force he once was, he was able to make a significant contribution for the next few years. In 1976, his final season with the Twins, he would play in 67 games and serve in a dual role as a player/coach.

He finished his career with a .304 average, 1,917 hits, 220 home runs, 329 doubles, 870 runs and 947 RBI.

Since his playing career ended, Oliva has continued to be involved with the Twins in a number of capacities. He has served multiple stints as a coach, instructor and consultant with the franchise. He is the only person to have served an on-field role in all three Twins World Series appearances. He has provided commentary on the Spanish-language Twins radio broadcasts for several years.

The Twins retired his No. 6 in 1991, making him the third player to have his number retired by the franchise. He was a member of the Twins inaugural Hall of Fame class in 2000 and was named to the Twins 40th Anniversary team in 2001. He was also one of four players honored with statues outside Target Field when the Twins' stadium opened in 2010.

While not elected to the National Baseball Hall of Fame as of this writing, Oliva's candidacy has been championed by several players of his era. In 2014, he missed getting elected by one vote in voting by the Golden Era Committee.

David Ortiz

DH/1B, Minnesota Twins (1997-2002)

There are few topics more likely to make a Twins fan curse than David Ortiz. It's well known that the Red Sox star and probable future Hall of Famer ("probable" only because of the voters' reluctance to add DHs to the Hall) spent several years with Minnesota before excelling for Boston.

Even more galling than a bad trade, of course, is that the Twins simply let him go rather than give him a raise with the slugger headed to arbitration. Instead, Twins fans had to watch from afar as Ortiz racked up home runs and postseason honors for the Sox.

The future "Big Papi" was born November 18, 1975, as David Américo Ortiz Arias, in Santo Domingo, Dominican Republic. The oldest of four children, Ortiz attended Estudia Espaillat High School in the Dominican Republic, and signed with the Seattle Mariners in 1992, shortly after his 17th birthday.

He made is his pro debut – as "David Arias" – with the Mariners' Arizona League rookie-level team in 1994, hitting .246 with two home runs in 53 games. He returned to play 48 games for the team in 1995, improving his average to .332.

That performance earned Arias/Ortiz a promotion to the Wisconsin Timber Rattlers of the Midwest League for 1996. In Wisconsin, Ortiz started to show some of that future power, hitting .322 with 18 home runs, 34 doubles and 93 RBI. That summer, he even wowed the local fans by outslugging Mariners stars Ken Griffey Jr. and Alex Rodriguez in a home run derby after a planned exhibition game with the big-league club was rained out. Ortiz also met his future wife in Wisconsin that summer.

Following his strong season, the Mariners sent Ortiz to the Twins as the "player to be named later" in an earlier trade for Dave Hollins.

After the trade, Ortiz informed the team that he wanted to be identified as David Ortiz, using his paternal family name.

Ortiz quickly worked his way up the ranks in 1997, starting the season with the A-level Fort Myers Miracle and ending it in Minnesota. Across three levels of the minors, he batted .317 with 31 home runs and 124 RBI. He made his major league debut with the Twins on September 2. He hit .327 in 15 games for the Twins that year and slugged his first major league home run on September 14 against the Texas Rangers.

Ortiz returned to the Twins in 1998, playing mostly at 1st base. After suffering a wrist injury in May, Ortiz ended up playing in only 86 games, hitting .277. The 1999 season didn't go much better, as Ortiz struggled in spring training and lost the 1st base job to Doug Mientkiewicz. Despite another strong season at AAA Salt Lake – a triple slash of .315/.412/.590 with 30 home runs and 110 RBI – Ortiz played only 10 games for the Twins.

The 2000 season found him back with the big-league club, where he hit .282 with 10 home runs, 26 doubles and 63 RBI in 130 games. Ortiz failed to build on that in 2001, though, when an injury again sidelined him for a good portion of the season, as he played in only 89 games hitting .234 with a career-high 18 home runs.

In what would turn out to be his final season with the Twins in 2002, Ortiz set career highs in home runs (20) and RBI (75), while hitting .272 and playing in 125 games. More importantly, the Twins returned to the postseason for the first time in more than a decade, winning the American League Central Division title. Ortiz delivered the decisive two-run double in Game 5 of that year's Division Series, helping the Twins move past the Oakland A's – the last postseason series win for Minnesota.

He finished his six years with the Twins with a .266 batting average and .461 slugging average and 58 home runs.

After the Twins made the ill-fated decision to release Ortiz following that season, his friend and fellow countryman Pedro Martinez lobbied the Red Sox to sign him. They agreed, and offered Ortiz a non-
guaranteed one-year contract. In Boston, Ortiz took uniform No. 34 in
honor of Twins great Kirby Puckett.

His success in Boston is well documented. He made an immediate
impact in 2003, hitting .288 with 31 home runs, 39 doubles and 101
RBI. He finished fifth in voting for the American League MVP award
– the first of five straight Top 5 finishes.

Ortiz went on to become a Boston legend, receiving 10 All-Star
nods and winning seven Silver Slugger awards. He led the American
League in RBI in 2005 and 2006, and also slugged a league-leading 54
home runs in '06. In his final season in 2016, he posted a .315 average,
and led the league in doubles, RBI and slugging at the age of 40. His 38
home runs that year are the most ever by a player in his final season.

And he was no postseason slouch, either. In 2004, when the Red
Sox ended their long championship drought, Ortiz batted .400 in the
postseason. He won the ALCS MVP award that year, hitting three
home runs with 11 RBI against the rival New York Yankees. He'd go on
to excel in the postseason as the Red Sox won additional titles in 2007
and 2013. His .688 average in the 2013 series against the St. Louis Cardinals would earn him the World Series MVP award. He also received
the Babe Ruth award for best postseason performance that season.

Ortiz finished his 20-year career with a .286 average, 2,472 hits,
632 doubles, 541 home runs, 1,768 RBI, 1,319 walks, a .380 on-base
percentage and .552 slugging average. In 85 postseason games, Ortiz
batted .289 with 17 home runs and 61 RBI, with a .404 OBP and .543
slugging average.

Ortiz was an eight-time winner of the Edgar Martinez Outstanding Designated Hitter award, two-time winner of the Hank Aaron
award, the 2010 Home Run Derby champion and winner of the 2011
Robert Clemente award. In 2009, Ortiz was named to all-decade teams

by both *Sports Illustrated* and *Sporting News*. The Red Sox retired his No. 34 in 2017.

Camilo Pascual

P, Minnesota Twins (1961-66)

When the Washington Senators moved to Minnesota in 1961, one of the few bright spots that first season was Camilo Pascual.

While the Twins finished 38 games out of first place, Pascual won 15 games and was the first Twins All-Star pitcher. He pitched three hitless innings and struck out four in the July 31 Midsummer Classic at Fenway Park.

Pascual was born January 20, 1934, in Havana, Cuba, one of three children. Older brother Carlos would also have a professional baseball career, pitching briefly for the Senators in 1950. His father, also Camilo, encouraged his children's interest in baseball, taking them to local games.

After years of playing on the local sandlots, Pascual made his pro debut at the age of 17 in 1951 in the Class D Oklahoma Sooner State League for the Chickasha Chiefs. He also pitched that summer for two Class C teams, the Big Spring Broncs and Geneva Robins. In the spring of 1952, he signed with the Senators, who assigned him to the Florida International League. He played for both the Havana Cubans and Tampa Smokers there, posting an 8-6 record in 24 games.

That winter (and until Castro closed the country in 1961), Pascual also began playing for various Cuban professional teams. He is generally regarded as one of the best pitchers in the history of the Cuban League, where he played six seasons, winning an MVP award for the 1955-56 season.

Back in the Florida International League, Pascual pitched another season for the Havana Cubans in 1953. He finished the year with a 10-6 record in 25 games. That performance was good enough to win Pascual an invite to spring training and a spot on the big-league club in 1954.

By the time Pascual joined the Senators, they were mired in a long, losing drought. The team hadn't won a pennant since 1933. In the 20 years between that success and Pascual's debut the team had only posted four winning seasons. While things wouldn't turn around until after the team moved to Minnesota, Pascual would be part of the team that would eventually bring a pennant to the franchise.

The team won 66 games in 1954, finishing 45 games out of first, but Pascual delivered a solid rookie season, finishing 4-7 with a 4.22 ERA, mostly pitching out of the bullpen. The team and Pascual continued to struggle for the next several years.

In 1959, the Senators were again relegated to irrelevancy, winning only 63 games, but the young core was starting to develop. Bob Allison won the Rookie of the Year Award and Harmon Killebrew had his breakout season, hitting 42 home runs to lead the American League. And Pascual posted the best season of his young career, pitching his way to a 17-10 record and 2.64 ERA. His 17 complete games and six shutouts both led the league and he earned his first All-Star nod that season.

Pascual started on Opening Day for the team's final season in Washington, and set a franchise record by striking out 15 batters. On a lousy Senators team that year, Pascual finished 12-8 with a 3.03 ERA and once again being named to the American League All-Star team.

His Minnesota debut was another All-Star year, as Pascual finished 15-16 with a 3.46 ERA. His eight shutouts and 221 strikeouts paced the American League. But it all started to come together for the Twins and Pascual in 1962.

The team found itself in a pennant race for the first time since World War II, winning 91 games and finishing in second place, only five games behind the New York Yankees. For Pascual, it was his first 20-win season, as he finished the year 20-11 with a 3.32 ERA, leading the league in complete games (18), shutouts (5) and strikeouts (206).

Pascual was even better in 1963, winning a career-high 21 games while dropping his ERA to 2.46. He again led the league with 18 complete games and 202 strikeouts. The team slipped to sixth place in 1964, but Pascual did win 15 games and earn his fifth and final All-Star selection.

The 1965 season ended up being one of the best in Twins history, as the team won 102 games and the American League pennant (still the only 100-win season for the Twins). But for Pascual, it was a disappointing season. Although he started the year 8-0, shoulder tightness and eventual surgery on that shoulder would cost him a good portion of the season. He finished 9-3, pitching only 156 innings. He would return to pitch in Game 3 of the World Series against the Los Angeles Dodgers. He lasted only five innings and took the loss for Twins, who lost the series in seven games to the Dodgers.

He struggled again in 1966 with shoulder pain and fatigue, pitching in 21 games. His eight wins and 4.89 ERA were his worst marks in a decade. That offseason, the Twins traded him to the new Washington Senators, making him one of only nine players to play for both versions of the team.

He won 25 games for Senators over the next two years, before the team released him after a dismal start to the 1969 season. He pitched briefly for the Cincinnati Reds, Dodgers and Cleveland Indians over the next couple seasons before retiring during the 1971 season.

He finished his career with a 174-170 record, 3.63 ERA, 132 complete games, 36 shutouts and 2,167 strikeouts. His 145 wins as a Senator/Twin are fifth-most in franchise history, while his 31 shutouts are second only to the legendary Walter Johnson.

Pascual retired to Miami, but returned to Minnesota in 1978 to serve as the pitching coach under Gene Mauch for three years. Since then, he has worked as a scout for a number of teams, signing a number of major leaguers including Jose Canseco and Alex Cora.

He was inducted into the Cuban Hall of Fame in 1983, the Caribbean Hall of Fame in 1996, the Latino Baseball Hall of Fame in 2010 and the Minnesota Twins Hall of Fame in 2012.

Gaylord Perry

G aylord Perry's older brother Jim (featured in the next profile) is a prominent alumnus of the Minnesota Twins, winning the 1970 Cy Young Award for the team.

What few people realize is that younger brother Gaylord also played in Minnesota. In fact, the future Hall of Famer started his professional career as a 19-year-old playing for the St. Cloud Rox of the Northern League, where his teammates included future All-Star Matty Alou. In his lone season with the Rox, Perry pitched in 17 games, finishing the season with a 9-5 record and 2.39 ERA.

But before any of that happened, Perry was growing up as the son of farmers in rural North Carolina. He was born Sept. 15, 1938, in Williamston, N.C., the second of three children. Father Evan was an athlete himself who reportedly turned down a contract to play minor league baseball and encouraged his sons to play the game.

Gaylord was a three-sport star at Williamson High School, winning All-State honors in football, leading his basketball team to the state tournament and capturing state titles in baseball. After an exhibition game staged for pro scouts, Perry was signed by the San Francisco Giants with a $60,000 bonus and three-year contract. The Giants assigned him to Class C St. Cloud for the 1958 season.

After his year in Minnesota, Perry worked his way up the minor league ranks for the next couple years. Perry pitched in Corpus Christi and Rio Grande Valley of the Texas League before spending the 1961 season with AAA Tacoma of the Pacific Coast League.

A strong spring training in 1962 resulted in Perry making the big-league club, and he made his major league debut for the Giants on April 14. He picked up his first win on April 25, but mostly struggled in his first stint with the Giants. After appearing in a few more games, Perry was sent back down to Tacoma. He returned to the Giants after the

PCL season ended, finishing the season with a 5.23 ERA in 13 games. The 1963 season was not much better, as Perry pitched in 31 games, mostly out of the bullpen.

After that season, though, the Giants made a fortuitous trade, acquiring pitcher Bob Shaw from the Milwaukee Braves. It was Shaw who, according to Perry, would teach the young pitcher how to throw a spitball. The spitter has been banned from the game since 1920, but many pitchers still found ways to doctor the ball using saliva, petroleum jelly or some other substance to improve its movement. Perry admitted in his 1974 book, *Me and the Spitter*, that he had used the practice – and also used the potential to psych out opposing batters.

Perry also worked with pitching coach Larry Jansen that spring to develop a slider. But whether it was the slider, the spitter or something else, Perry made a big step forward in 1964. Splitting his time between the rotation and bullpen, Perry finished the season 12-11 with a 2.75 ERA.

After a step back in 1965, Perry rang up his first 20-win season in 1966. That year ended with a 21-8 record, 2.99 ERA and 13 complete games in 35 starts. It was also Perry's first selection for an All-Star team. He finished second to Sandy Koufax in voting for *The Sporting News* Pitcher of the Year award.

Perry continued to pitch well for the Giants for the next few years, but didn't top the 20-win mark again until finishing 23-13 in 1970. His five shutouts and 328 2/3 innings led the National League and Perry earned another All-Star berth, while finishing second to Bob Gibson of the St. Louis Cardinals in Cy Young balloting. His 23 wins tied Gibson for the league lead. Along with Jim's 20 wins for the Twins, that made the Perrys the first brothers to win 20 games in the same season.

Perry was also getting attention for the widely held belief (but still not confirmed at that point) that he was cheating. Baseball cracked down on the spitball, but to no avail as pitchers continued to get more creative. Perry, despite being challenged repeatedly, was yet to be caught.

After a 16-win season in 1971 (in which he surrendered Hank Aaron's 600th home run), the Giants traded Perry to the Cleveland Indians. The change of scenery seemed to benefit Perry, as he finally won that elusive Cy Young award. He posted a career-best 1.92 ERA, while winning a career-high and league-leading 24 games. His 29 complete games also paced the junior circuit and Perry was selected for his third All-Star team. His Cy Young win made the Perrys the only brothers to win Cy Young awards.

Perry would win 19 games in 1973. On July 3, he pitched against brother Jim for the only time in the regular season (Gaylord took the loss). Perry won 21 games in 1974, again appearing in the All-Star Game. The 1974 season was also special, as Jim joined the team in a March trade. Both players started the 1975 season with Cleveland, but Jim was traded to Oakland in May.

After a 6-9 start to the season – and frequent clashes with new manager Frank Robinson – Gaylors was traded to the Texas Rangers. Perry spent the next two-and-a-half years with the Rangers, posting double-digit win totals each year until they traded him to the San Diego Padres in February 1978.

At 39 years old, Perry was back in the National League. It was a welcome return, as Perry won his second Cy Young award, finishing 21-6 with a 2.73 ERA. The 1979 season in San Diego was not nearly as successful for Perry, despite making his fifth and final All-Star team. By the end of the year, Perry had quit the team and threatened to retire unless they traded him back to the Rangers. The Padres finally gave in in February, returning Perry to the American League.

Perry pitched well for the Rangers, but had only a 6-9 record for the struggling team. On August 24, the Rangers sent Perry to the New York Yankees, where he would finish the season 4-4 for the eventual American League East Division Champions. The Yankees released the 42-year-old following the season, and he signed with the Atlanta Braves. Perry would only win eight games in the strike-shortened 1981 season, leaving him just three short of 300 for his career.

He struggled to find a team for the 1982 season before signing on with the Seattle Mariners in March 1982. On May 6 of that year, he finally picked up that 300th win, a complete game victory over the Yankees. He pitched his way to a 10-12 record and 4.40 ERA in 32 starts. But perhaps more notably, the long-suspected Perry was finally caught throwing illegal pitches in an August 23 game against the Boston Red Sox.

Perry returned to the Mariners in 1983, winning three games before the team released him in June. He signed on with the Kansas City Royals in July, making 14 starts and winning four games. Perry retired after the 1983 season, shortly after his 45th birthday.

Perry finished his career with a 314-265 record, 3.11 ERA, 303 complete games, 53 shutouts and 3,534 strikeouts (third-highest at the time of his retirement). He was elected to the Hall of Fame in 1991, and was a finalist for the Major League Baseball All-Century Team. In 1999, *The Sporting News* ranked him No. 97 on its list of Baseball's 100 Greatest Players of the 20th Century. The Giants retired his No. 36 in 2005.

Jim Perry

P, Minnesota Twins (1963-72)

Hall of Famer Gaylord Perry may be the better-known Perry to most of the baseball world, but to a certain generation of Twins fans, it is Jim who will always hold a special place in their hearts.

Perry not only won the 1970 American League Cy Young award – the first in Twins history – but he was also a key member of the pennant- and division-winning teams of the late 1960s.

Born October 30, 1935, in Williamston, N.C., Perry was the oldest of three children of a farming family. Besides younger brother Gaylord's success on the diamond, baseball appears to have been in the Perry genes, as father Evan was also an accomplished local player.

Perry pitched on the Williamston High School baseball team, leading the team to a state championship his senior year. After high school, he attended Campbell College, where he was signed by the Cleveland Indians before the 1956 season.

Perry made his pro debut in 1956, pitching for the North Platte Indians of the Nebraska State League. He posted a 7-8 record and 4.80 ERA in 16 games for the Class D team. He quickly moved up the minor league ranks, playing for the Fargo-Moorhead Twins in 1957 and the Reading Indians in 1958.

After a strong performance in spring training in 1959, Perry made the jump from A ball to the big leagues. He started out the season in the bullpen, but moved into the rotation in the second half of the season to replace the injured Herb Score – joining another future Twin, Mudcat Grant. In 44 games (13 starts), Perry finished 12-10, with a 2.65 ERA, eight complete games, two shutouts and four saves. It was a good enough performance for Perry to finish second in American League Rookie of the Year voting to Washington Senator and future Twins teammate Bob Allison.

Perry moved into the rotation in 1960, winning a league-leading 18 games – but also giving up a league-leading 35 home runs. He slumped to a 10-17 record in 1961 and led the league in earned runs allowed (but did receive his first All-Star selection). 1962 wasn't much better, with Perry finishing 12-12 with a 4.14 ERA.

New Indians Manager Birdie Tebbetts moved Perry to the bullpen to start the 1963 season. On May 2, after Perry had pitched in only five games and posted a 5.23 ERA, the Indians sent him to the Twins for fellow pitcher Jack Kralick. (Kralick, incidentally, would win 33 games for the Indians over the next five seasons, while Perry would end up winning 128 in his 10 years with the Twins.)

Perry found new life with the Twins and finishing 9-9 with a 3.74 ERA. Perry spent the 1964 season and the first half of the 1965 season pitching out of the bullpen for the Twins. The team moved him to the rotation in July and Perry was a key part of that year's World Series team, winning 12 games with a 2.63 ERA.

Perry continued to bounce back and forth between the rotation and bullpen for the next several years, filling key roles on the pitching staff. He spent most of the 1969 season in the rotation, a move that paid off for the Twins as Perry finished 20-6 with a 2.82 ERA in 46 games. He finished third in voting for the Cy Young award, and ninth in voting for the MVP as the Twins won the newly formed American League West division. In his lone postseason start against the eventual AL Champion Baltimore Orioles, he gave up three runs in eight innings of a Twins loss.

Perry followed that up with a 24-12 record in 1970, even as his ERA climbed to 3.04 in his league-leading 40 starts. That season earned him the American League Cy Young award and his second All-Star berth. The Twins again won the division, and again lost to the Orioles in the ALCS. Perry was shelled in his lone start, giving up three home runs and eight runs total in 5 1/3 innings.

Perry's 1971 season was a mixed bag. He was selected for the All-Star Game again, but also finished 17-17 as the Twins fell to fifth place. He surrendered 39 home runs, the most in the league. He lowered his ERA by almost a run in 1972 to 3.35, but his record dropped to 13-16 and the Twins were again out of the pennant race.

At the end of spring training in 1973, the Twins traded Perry to the Detroit Tigers for pitcher Danny Fife. Perry finished the season 14-13. That year, he also pitched against brother Gaylord for the only time, a 5-4 victory for the Tigers (although Jim had a no-decision). Perry was again traded at the end of spring training in 1974, this time going to the Indians, where he joined Gaylord.

The brothers made a good team for the Indians in 1974, with Jim finishing 17-12 with a 2.96 ERA and Gaylord winning 21 games. The brothers accounted for almost half of the Indians 77 wins that year. Jim won his 200th career game that summer. That 1974 season ended up being Jim's last hurrah of sorts, as the 1975 season was not so kind. He started out the season 1-6 for the Indians with a 6.69 ERA in eight games. The Indians traded him to the Oakland Athletics on May 20 (and sent Gaylord to the Texas Rangers a few weeks later). After Perry posted a 3-4 record in 15 games for the A's, the team released him in August and Perry retired as a player.

He finished his career with a 215-174 record, 3.45 ERA, 109 complete games, 32 shutouts and 308 home runs surrendered in 630 games. He won 128 of those games in a Twins uniform – fifth most in team history. He's also in the Top 10 for his Twins career in innings pitched, win/loss percentage, strikeouts, games started and shutouts.

Following his retirement, Perry worked for several years as a scout for the A's. In 2011, the Twins inducted Perry into the team Hall of Fame.

Kirby Puckett

OF, Minnesota Twins (1984-95)

For those who grew up watching the Twins during their World Series heyday, there was no bigger star than Kirby Puckett. He was the face of the franchise in the 1980s and 1990s on the way to his Hall of Fame career.

It all started with much humbler beginnings, though. Puckett was born March 14, 1960, in Chicago, the youngest of nine children. He grew up in the Robert Taylor Homes, a public housing project on the city's south side. Puckett played third base for Calumet High School, but with his only scholarship offer being from a Florida junior college, Puckett opted to stay in Chicago and work at the local Ford plant.

As Puckett wrote in his 1993 autobiography, if it wasn't for the hiring practices of Ford, he might never have played professional baseball. Tired of going to school, he was happy to be working for Ford, but the company had a policy that employees could work for 90 days without becoming union employees. According to Puckett, he was let go on his 89th day.

Working temp jobs and looking for a future path, Puckett decided to attend a major-league baseball tryout camp. While no contract offer came from the tryout, Puckett did catch the eye of Dewey Kalmer, baseball coach at Bradley University. Kalmer offered Puckett a full scholarship to come down to Peoria, IL, to play for the Braves.

As Puckett was starting his college career in the fall of 1980, his father died, and Puckett returned to Chicago for several weeks. When baseball season started, Puckett struggled to get on to the field with Bradley's experienced infield. It was Kalmer who had the idea of moving Puckett to the outfield, where he shone in his lone year with the Braves. Puckett earned all-conference honors that spring, but his absence following his father's death had left him behind in classes. Rather than attend summer school to stay eligible, Puckett decided to move closer to home and transferred to Triton Junior College.

In a fateful decision, though, he spent the summer of 1981 playing in the Central Illinois Collegiate League. That's where he caught the eye of Minnesota Twins scout Jim Rantz. With major-league baseball players on strike that summer, most organizations were shut down, so Rantz had the chance to go see his son play in the summer college league. Playing for the other team was one Kirby Puckett.

The Twins selected Puckett with their first pick in the January 1982 draft. After his season with Triton – which earned Puckett Junior College Player of the Year honors for the region – Puckett signed with the Twins. He made his pro debut that summer, playing 65 games for the Rookie-level Elizabethton Twins. He hit .382, with only three home runs, but 43 stolen bases, and was named the league's player of the year by *Baseball America*.

The Twins promoted Puckett to the Class A Visalia Oaks in 1983, where he had another standout season. In 138 games in the California League, Puckett hit .314, with nine home runs, 29 doubles, 93 RBI and 48 stolen bases.

Puckett made the jump to AAA baseball in 1984, starting out the season with Toledo of the International League. After 24 games with the Mud Hens, Puckett got the call to play for the Twins. He made his debut on May 8 against the California Angels, collecting four hits in his first game. In 128 games in the big leagues, Puckett hit .296, with 12 doubles and 14 stolen bases. He finished third in voting for the American League Rookie of the Year award.

The 1985 season found Puckett among the league leaders in hits, triples and at-bats, but he was still lacking power, adding only four home runs. After the 1985 season, Puckett worked with Twins hitting coach Tony Oliva and developed a leg kick that made a big difference in his power output.

That 1986 season saw Puckett rack up a triple slash of .328/.366/.537. He hit a career-high 31 home runs, adding 37 doubles and 96 RBI. He finished in the top five in the American League in average, hits, at-bats, runs and total bases. He earned the first of six Silver Slugger awards, the first of his six Gold Gloves and the first of 10 straight All-Star selections. He finished sixth in MVP voting, one of seven times he would finish in the Top 10 in the American League MVP race.

The 1987 season was big one for the Twins and Puckett. For Puckett, it was another All-Star, Gold Glove and Silver Slugger season. His 207 hits tied for the league lead, while his .332 average was good for fourth. He added 28 home runs and 99 RBI as the Twins won the American League West. The underdog Twins defeated the Detroit Tigers in the American League Championship Series. They defeated the St. Louis Cardinals in the World Series in seven games, with Puckett hitting .357 with a team-leading 10 hits.

Puckett had a career year in 1988, setting career highs in batting average (.356), hits (234), RBI (121) and slugging average (.545). He led the league in hits, at bats and total bases. He was second in the AL in batting, RBI and doubles, while adding 24 home runs. He collected his 1,000th hit during the 1988 season – only the fourth player to do so in his first five seasons. His .356 average was the highest recorded by an AL righthander since Joe DiMaggio hit .357 in 1941.

Puckett again led the league in hits in 1989, with 215, and this time added a batting title. His .339 average made him the third Twin to win a batting title after Tony Oliva and Rod Carew. He was also only the third batter to lead the AL in hits for three straight years, joining Oliva and Ty Cobb.

After the 1989 season, Puckett signed a 3-year/$9 million contract extension that briefly made him the highest-paid player in baseball. Puckett had an off-season – by his standards – in 1990, with his average dropping to .298 with only 164 hits in 146 games. The Twins dropped to the cellar in the AL West as well.

Both rebounded in 1991, though, as the Twins made their magical run from last place to the World Series. Puckett batted .319, with another All-Star selection and his fifth Gold Glove. In the ALCS, Puckett won the MVP award as he hit .429 with two home runs and the Twins beat the Toronto Blue Jays in five games.

In the World Series, the Twins faced off against the Atlanta Braves, another worst-to-first team. It was a classic seven-game battle that many have called the greatest World Series ever. While Puckett's overall numbers weren't great (a .250 average), it was Game Six that cemented his status as a Twins legend. In the first inning he tripled in a run (and later scored himself). In the third inning, with a runner on base, Puckett made a leaping catch in front of the Metrodome's plexiglass to rob Ron Gant of an extra base hit. Then, leading off the 11th inning, Puckett hit the game-winning home run off of the Braves' Charlie Liebrandt, forever etching in Twins lore the call by Jack Buck, "And we'll see you tomorrow night!"

That World Series win would end up being the last time the Twins made the playoffs during Puckett's career, although Puckett continued to have several more good seasons for the team. In 1992, Puckett hit .329, leading the league with 210 hits and 313 total bases, along with 19 home runs and 110 RBI. He won his sixth and final Gold Glove award and finished second in voting for the AL MVP to Oakland reliever Dennis Eckersley.

After his All-Star season in 1993 (and an All-Star Game MVP award) Puckett was in the midst of another good year in 1994 when the players' strike prematurely ended the season. In 108 games, his 112 RBI led the league. Along with a .317 average, Puckett was among the league leaders in at-bats, hits, total bases and doubles. He racked up his 2,000th career hit that season, as well as hit No. 2,086, moving him ahead of Rod Carew for the No. 1 spot in Twins history.

1995 seemed like another good season for Puckett, as he hit .314, with 23 home runs and 99 RBI, and collecting his 200th career home run. However, it would end early when Puckett was hit by a pitch in the face from Dennis Martinez that broke his jaw.

Puckett was recovered and ready to go in spring training in 1996, looking like his old self. But on March 28, Puckett woke up with blurred vision in his right eye. He was diagnosed with glaucoma and despite treatment and surgeries, the vision did not return. On July 12, 1996, Puckett announced his retirement. He won the Roberto Clemente Award for community service after the 1996 season.

For his career, Puckett hit .318, with 2,304 hits, 1,071 runs, 414 doubles, 207 home runs and 1,085 RBI in 12 seasons. He has more hits and singles than any other Twin, and ranks among the career Twins leaders in batting average, slugging percentage, OPS, at-bats, runs scored, total bases, home runs and RBI.

The Twins retired his No. 34 in 1997, and in 1999 he was ranked No. 86 on The Sporting News list of the 100 Greatest Baseball Players. He was part of the inaugural class of the Twins Hall of Fame in 2000, and was elected to the Baseball Hall of Fame in his first year of eligibility in 2001.

Off the field, though, retirement did not go easy for the former Twins star. Multiple reports surfaced beginning in 2002, alleging domestic abuse and other misconduct by Puckett. He was also accused of groping a woman in a restaurant bathroom in 2002 and faced several charges, although he was found not guilty in a 2003 trial.

After being a very visible part of the Twins organization for years, Puckett moved to Scottsdale, AZ, in 2003. On March 5, 2006, he suffered a stroke at his home there. He died the next day at the age of 45. More than 15,000 Twins fans braved a winter storm to attend a memorial at the Metrodome a week later.

When Target Field opened in 2010, Puckett was among the Twins legends immortalized with a statue on the Target Plaza. Gate 34 at the stadium is also named in his honor.

Brad Radke

P, Minnesota Twins (1995-2006)

I f there's one thing that most baseball fans remember about Brad Radke, it's his propensity to give up home runs – immortalized in a 1990s commercial for Sega Sports World Series Baseball II. The commercial is still readily available online for those readers that are interested.

Such was the fate of an underrated pitcher that had the bad luck to pitch for the abysmal Twins teams of the 1990s.

Radke was born October 27, 1972, in Eau Claire, WI, a short drive from his future big-league home. His family moved to Florida when Radke was a child, and he first caught the attention of scouts while pitching for Jesuit High School in Tampa. Radke played both basketball – as the team's go-to three-point shooter – and baseball. (His son Kasey would go on to pitch the championship game when the school won the 2014 state title.)

The Twins selected Radke in the eighth round of the 1991 amateur draft and assigned him to the rookie-level GCL Twins. In 10 games in the Gulf Coast League, he finished 3-4 with a 3.08 ERA. For his first full season in professional baseball in 1992, the Twins sent him to the Midwest League. Radke pitched in 26 games for the Kenosha Twins, winning 10 and posting a 2.93 ERA, while striking out 127 batters.

After starting the 1993 season with the Fort Myers Miracle, Radke was promoted to the AA Nashville Xpress at midseason. He returned to Nashville in 1994, where his 12-9 season (and 2.66 ERA) was good enough to earn him an invite to spring training in 1995. Radke made the jump to the majors that year on the increasingly young (and struggling) Twins.

When Radke joined the Twins, the team was in the midst of an eight-year run of irrelevancy that would go on to include Kirby Puckett's retirement, Chuck Knoblauch's forcing a trade, a threatened move to North Carolina and the specter of contraction. Only four years removed from a World Series title, the Twins finished the season 56-88, 44 games out of first place in the American League Central.

Radke did finish ninth in voting for the Rookie of the Year award as teammate Marty Cordova won the honor, but overall the season was a struggle. He finished 11-14 with a 5.32 ERA and surrendered a league-leading 32 home runs. He improved slightly in 1996, again winning 11 games, but dropping his ERA to 4.46. He did give up 40 home runs that year, once again tops in the American League.

1997 would prove to be Radke's career year as he posted his only 20-win season finishing the year 20-10 in a league-leading 35 starts. That summer, he won 12 consecutive starts, becoming only the third pitcher to accomplish that feat since 1950. He finished the season third in voting for the Cy Young Award. While he won only 12 games in 1998, Radke did earn his only All-Star selection that summer. Radke also won 12 games in the 1999 and 2000 seasons.

In 2001, the young Twins team surprised most of baseball by jumping out to an early lead in the American League Central. While the Twins would eventually finish second to the Cleveland Indians, the team's 85 wins was the most since 1992. Radke, now the veteran leader of the rotation, finished the season with a 15-11 record and 3.94 ERA. His average of only one walk per nine innings was the best in the American League.

The Twins finally returned to the playoffs in 2002, winning the division. Radke was limited, twice heading to the disabled list with a groin injury and pitched in only 21 games, winning nine. Radke started two games in the Twins Division Series win over the Oakland Athletics, winning both while posting a 1.54 ERA. He pitched well in his lone start against the Anaheim Angels in the American League Championship Series, but took the loss as the Twins offense struggled. Radke won 14 games in 2003 and 11 games in 2004 as the Twins won two more division titles (but lost to the New York Yankees in the playoffs both years).

After a disappointing 2005 season when the Twins finished in third place and Radke won only nine games, both rebounded in 2006. The first two months gave no indication the Twins had another run in them, though. As of June 7, the Twins were sitting at 25-33, 11.5 games behind the Detroit Tigers and mired in fourth place. The team went on a tear, winning 9 of its next 10 games to get back to .500. Over the next three months, the Twins played excellent baseball and, on the final day of the season, caught the Tigers to win the division.

As for Radke, he pitched the season with a torn labrum. From June through September he went 8-3 with a 2.68 ERA in 17 starts. In August, he suffered a stress fracture in his shoulder, but returned to the team in September, making his final Metrodome start September 28. He was in so much pain that he had to undertake everyday activities with his non-pitching left arm. After the Twins were swept by the A's, Radke announced his retirement.

In his 12-year career with the Twins, Radke was 148-139 with a 4.22 ERA in 378 games. His 148 wins are third-most in Twins history, and he's also in the Twins Top five in BB/9 innings, innings pitched, strikeouts and games started – and No. 1 in home runs allowed.

Radke was elected to the Twins Hall of Fame in 2009 and named to the team's All-Metrodome team that same year.

Johan Santana

P, Minnesota Twins (2000-07)

I t's quite simply one of the best acquisitions in Twins history. On December 13, 1999, the Twins chose pitcher Jared Camp with the first pick of the Rule 5 draft. They immediately dealt Camp to the Florida Marlins in a pre-arranged trade for Johan Santana, taken second in the draft, and $50,000.

Camp would never make it out of the minor leagues, while Santana would go on to be one of the best pitchers in Twins history. The Twins thought he could be a solid pitcher, but had no idea of just how could he would become: "I'd really love to revise history and tell you we thought he was going to be the greatest pitcher in Twins history," Mike Radcliff, the Twins scouting director at the time, told MLB.com in 2017.

Johan Santana was born March 13, 1979, in Tovar, Venezuela, a coffee-growing town in the Andes Mountains. His father, Jesus, was a talented ballplayer in his own right, who was reportedly courted by professional Venezuelan teams. Johan would play as an infielder, outfielder and pitcher on local teams before catching the eye of scout Andres Reimer at a 1994 tournament. Reimer brought him to the Houston Astros Venezuelan academy in 1995, where Santana became a full-time pitcher.

The 17-year-old pitched in the Dominican League in 1996 before coming stateside to pitch for the Astros Gulf Coast League rookie-level team in 1997. In his first season in the U.S., Santana pitched in nine games and posted a 7.93 ERA.

His numbers improved in 1998 as he split the season between two A-level teams, the Auburn Doubledays of the New York-Penn League and Quad Cities River Bandits of the Midwest League. In 17 games, Santana finished with a 7-6 record and 4.73 ERA, while also striking out 94 in 93 innings. He returned to the Midwest League in 1999, pitching in 27 games for the Michigan White Caps, finishing 8-8 with a 4.66 ERA and 150 strikeouts.

The Astros chose not to protect Santana in the 1999 Rule 5 minor league draft, giving the Twins the chance to acquire him. Under the rules of the draft, the Twins were required to keep Santana on the major league club for the entire 2000 season. Santana pitched in 30 games, and started five, for the last-place Twins that season, posting a 6.49 ERA in 86 innings pitched.

Santana returned to the Twins in 2001, but was limited to 15 games with a flexor pronator strain. In 43 innings, he finished 1-0 with a 4.74 ERA. He started the 2002 season with the AAA Edmonton Trappers, where he worked with coach Bobby Cuellar on his changeup, the pitch that would become is signature.

That work paid immediate dividends when Santana returned to the Twins on May 31. In 27 games (14 starts), Santana posted an 8-6 record, 2.99 ERA and 137 strikeouts in only 108 innings. He did lead the league with 15 wild pitches, though, and struggled in the postseason, giving up six runs in 6 1/3 innings.

Santana once again started the season in the bullpen in 2003. His success there – and struggles of the Twins' starters – led to Santana landing in the rotation for good in July. He finished the season 12-3 in 45 games, with a 3.07 ERA and 169 strikeouts. Santana also finished seventh in voting for the American League Cy Young award. With a great second half, the Twins rallied to win their second straight division title. Santana got the nod to start Game 1 of the American League Division Series against the New York Yankees and held them scoreless for four innings before a leg cramp forced him from the game. The Twins would win that game, but the Yankees tagged Santana for six runs in 3 2/3 innings in Game 4 to clinch the series.

In 2004, Santana was finally made a full-time starter, beginning one of the greatest three-year runs for a pitcher. But it didn't start that way after Santana underwent offseason surgery for bone chips in his elbow.

At the end of May, Santana was sitting with an ERA north of 5 and a 2-4 record. On June 9, Santana struck out 10 New York Mets, starting an 18-2 run over his final 22 starts. Over that time, in 159 1/3 innings, Santana posted a 1.36 ERA and 204 strikeouts. Twelve times he reached double digits in strikeouts.

For the season, Santana finished 20-6, leading the league in ERA (2.61), strikeouts (265) WHIP (.921), WAR (8.6) and strikeouts/9 innings (10.5). He won his first Cy Young award and finished sixth in MVP balloting. In the playoffs, Santana pitched seven scoreless innings in the Twins Game 1 win against the Yankees (the last postseason win to date for the Twins). He held the Yankees to one run in his Game 4 start, but the bullpen blew a 5-1 lead as the Twins again lost to New York in the playoffs.

The Twins slipped to third place in 2005, and Santana again started the season slowly. A strong second half helped Santana finish 16-7 with a 2.87 ERA, a league-leading 238 strikeouts and his first All-Star berth. Santana also finished third in voting for the Cy Young Award. The argument can certainly be made that in the modern era, Santana would have won the award that year. The only statistical category in which winner Bartolo Colon of the Los Angeles Angels bettered Santana was his 21 wins.

The Twins and Santana would bounce back in 2006, with the Twins winning another division title, and Santana winning the pitching triple crown with a 19-6 record, 2.77 ERA and 245 strikeouts, while leading the league in a number of other categories and making his second All-Star team. That won him his second unanimous Cy Young Award. In his lone postseason start, he gave up only two runs in eight innings, but still lost as the Twins offense struggled against Oakland.

The 2007 season would end up being the Twins first losing one since 2000, and Santana slipped as well. He finished 15-13 with a 3.33 ERA, while giving up a league-leading 33 home runs. He still struck out 235 batters in 219 innings, garnering his third All-Star nod and winning his only Gold Glove. On August 19, he struck out 17 batters against the Texas Rangers, setting the Twins' single-game record.

With little chance of re-signing Santana, the Twins began shopping him around to other teams following the 2007 season. After discussions with the Yankees and Red Sox, the Twins dealt Santana to the New York Mets for four players: outfielder Carlos Gomez and pitchers Philip Humber, Deolis Guerra and Kevin Mulvey. None of them ended up making much of an impact for the Twins, although Gomez would be a Gold Glove winner and two-time All Star with the Milwaukee Brewers and Humber pitched a perfect game for the Chicago White Sox in 2012.

Santana signed a record-setting $137.5 million extension with the Mets and rewarded the team with a solid 2008. His 2.53 ERA led the league as he won 16 games and struck out 206 batters, despite a torn meniscus in his left knee. He had surgery during the offseason, but injuries would continue to plague him.

Santana started out strong in 2009, making another All-Star team, but was shut down in August for surgery to remove bone chips from his elbow. That year, he was also named to the Twins' All-Metrodome team.

In 2010, Santana pitched well through September, winning 11 games with a 2.98 ERA. After Santana experienced shoulder discomfort in his final start, an MRI found a torn anterior capsule in his left shoulder. The surgery and recovery caused him to miss the entire 2011 season.

Santana returned to the Mets in 2012, starting on opening day. On June 1, he pitched the first no-hitter in Mets history, but threw a career-high 134 pitches to get it. That game has been blamed by many for what followed. As it turned out, Santana would only make 10 more starts in his career, pitching to an 8.27 ERA. In July, Santana returned to the disabled list, this time with a sprained ankle. In August, it was a inflammation in his lower back.

In 2013, he tore his shoulder capsule for the second time. After the Mets bought out his contract, Santana attempted several comebacks, but suffered a myriad of injuries. He finally announced his retirement in 2018, the same year he was inducted into the Twins Hall of Fame.

For his 12-year career, Santana finished 139-78, with a 3.20 ERA and 1,988 strikeouts in 360 games. His 8.833 strikeouts per nine innings is 20th best in baseball history and .641 winning percentage is the 37th highest, as of the 2019 season. As a Twin, his .679 winning percentage and 9.497 strikeouts per nine innings are tops in team history.

Duke Snider

OF, St. Paul Saints (1947)

O n June 13, 1956, the Brooklyn Dodgers came to Minnesota for an exhibition game against the St. Paul Saints of the American Association. The Dodgers won 7-2 as five players, including Duke Snider, hit home runs. For the Hall of Fame outfielder, it was a return to the Twin Cities, where he had played 66 games for the Saints in 1947.

Edwin Donald Snider was born Sept. 19, 1926, in Los Angeles, receiving the nickname Duke as a child. Snider played baseball, football and basketball at Compton High School and was signed by the Dodgers even before he graduated high school in 1944.

The 17-year-old Snider batted .294 in 131 games for the Class B Newport News Dodgers that year, along with two hitless at-bats for the AA Montreal Royals. Snider missed the 1945 season serving in the U.S. Navy. After completing 19 months of military service, Snider returned to the Dodgers organization in June 1946, where he played 68 games for the Fort Worth Cats.

Snider earned an invitation to spring training from the Dodgers in 1947 and started the season with the big-league club. In early July, the Dodgers sent Snider down to St. Paul. In 66 games with the Saints, Snider batted .316 with a .584 slugging average, 12 home runs and 46 RBI. Snider rejoined the Dodgers in time for the World Series that year, although he didn't play in the postseason.

After splitting the 1948 season between Montreal and Brooklyn, Snider became a fixture in the Dodgers lineup in 1949, hitting .292 with 23 home runs. Snider had his breakout season in 1950, hitting .321 with 31 home runs, 31 doubles, 107 RBI and a league-leading 199 hits. He also earned his first All-Star selection that season, the first of seven straight All-Star years for the Dodgers star.

The 1952 season saw the Dodgers returning to the World Series against the New York Yankees. While the Dodgers lost in seven games, Snider hit .345 with four home runs. Snider had the best stretch of his career starting in 1953, hitting at least 40 home runs for five straight seasons. In 1953, he hit .336 with 42 home runs and 126 RBI, while leading the league with 132 runs and a .627 slugging average and finishing third in MVP voting. His .341/.423/.647 triple slash in 1954, with 40 home runs and 130 RBI, and a league-leading 120 runs, garnered a fourth-place finish in MVP voting.

The 1955 season was another strong one for Snider, with a .309/.418/.628, 42 home runs, and league-leading totals of 126 runs and 136 RBI. He finished a close second to teammate Roy Campanella in MVP voting in 1955 as the Dodgers finally won a World Series over the rival Yankees. Snider hit .320 with four home runs, making him the only player to hit four home runs in two different World Series. Snider won *The Sporting News* National League Player of the Year Award for his outstanding season.

Snider led the league in home runs for the only time in his career in 1956, with 43 long balls. His .399 on-base percentage and .598 slugging also led the National League. Snider added another 40 home run season in 1957, the Dodgers' final year in Brooklyn.

After the Dodgers moved to Los Angeles, Snider struggled with an aching knee and saw his offensive numbers decline. After the 1962 season, Snider returned to New York when the Dodgers sold his rights to the Mets. Playing for the worst team in baseball, Snider was selected for one final All-Star Game in 1963. He also had two other career highlights that season: on April 16, he recorded his 2,000[th] career hit and on June 14 he slugged his 400th career home run.

Snider was sold to the San Francisco Giants on opening day of 1964 after requesting a trade to a contending team. In 91 games, he hit .210 with four home runs in his return to the West Coast. Snider retired after the 1964 season.

For his career, Snider hit .295, with a .380 OBP, .540 slugging average, 2,116 hits, 358 doubles, 407 home runs and 1,333 RBI. In 36 World Series games, Snider batted .286 with 11 home runs.

Following his retirement, Snider worked as a television and radio announcer for the San Diego Padres and Montreal Expos. He was elected to the Hall of Fame in 1980. That same year, the Dodgers retired his uniform No. 4. In 1999, he was ranked No. 84 on The Sporting News list of 100 Greatest Players, and was a nominee for Major League Baseball's All-Century Team.

Snider died on February 27, 2011, at the age of 84 in Escondido, CA.

Jim Thome

DH, Minnesota Twins (2010-11)

J im Thome's time at Target Field may have been brief, but his 179 games with the Minnesota made an outsized impression on Thome as well as the Twins.

Thome helped inaugurate Target Field in 2010 with 25 home runs, serving as the designated hitter on Minnesota's most recent division champs. In 2011, he added 12 more home runs – including career No. 600. For Thome, it was a special time, too.

"I loved the state of Minnesota," he told the St. Paul Pioneer Press in 2018. "Being an outdoorsman, it fit me so well at that time of my career. And the driving force for me after the first year was to make sure I went back there to be able to hit that milestone of 600."

Meeting Twins legend Harmon Killebrew was a highlight for Thome, he told the paper: "I don't think you'd meet a finer man than Harmon. I never had a chance to really meet Stan Musial, but you hear stories that two of the finest men that ever put a uniform on were Harmon and Stan."

Thome was born August 27, 1970, in Peoria, IL, the youngest of five children. He earned all-state honors in baseball and basketball at Limestone High School. Thome graduated from high school in 1988 and, after going undrafted, enrolled in Illinois Central College, where he played both baseball and basketball. After one season at ICC, the Cleveland Indians selected Thome in the 13th round of the 1989 draft.

Thome made his pro debut that year, playing 55 games for the Rookie-level GCL Indians. He finished the season with a .237 average and no home runs. After that season, Thome met coach and future Cleveland skipper Charlie Manuel, who helped Thome adjust his swing.

The changes paid off immediately for Thome, who hit .340/.466/.609 with 16 home runs and 50 RBI in 67 minor league games in 1990. He followed that up with another successful season in 1991, earning a September call-up with the Indians. He made his major league debut September 4, recording two hits against the Twins.

Injuries limited Thome for the 1992 season, which he split between AAA and the big leagues. He spent most of the 1993 season with the AAA Charlotte Knights, where he led the International League with a .332 average, adding 25 home runs and 102 RBI. He joined the Indians for the end of the season, hitting .266 with seven home runs and 22 RBI in 47 games.

Starting with the 1994 season, Thome would be a key part of the Indians run of contending teams. In 1995, Thome hit .314/.438/.558 with 25 home runs and 73 RBI as the Indians advanced to the World Series, losing to the Atlanta Braves. He broke out in a big way in 1996 when his .311/.450/.612 triple slash, along with 38 home runs and 166 RBI earned him his first Silver Slugger award.

That 1996 season was the first of nine seasons in a row (and 12 for his career) with at least 30 home runs. 1997 saw Thome earn the first of five All-Star selections as the Indians again lost the World Series. In his first 12 years with the Indians, he led the league in walks three times and strikeouts twice. In 2002, he set an Indians club record with 52 home runs, while leading the league with a .677 slugging average.

After the 2002 season, Thome signed a six-year $85 million free-agent contract with the Philadelphia Phillies. In his first year with the club, he hit a league-leading 47 home runs with 131 RBI. He was also recognized with the Lou Gehrig Memorial Award, which recognizes players for their character and integrity.

His second season with Philadelphia was a disappointment, as Thome missed most of the season with injuries. Ryan Howard, his replacement at first base, excelled in Thome's absence, winning the National League Rookie of the Year award. With Thome now expendable, the Phillies sent him to the Chicago White Sox on November 25, 2005.

In his first season in Chicago, Thome slugged 42 home runs while earning an All-Star selection. He followed that up with 35 home runs – including career No. 500 – in 2007, and 34 home runs in 2008. In the one-game playoff against the Twins that year, his home run was the deciding factor in Chicago's 1-0 victory. After he hit 23 home runs through 107 games in 2009, the White Sox traded him to the Los Angeles Dodgers for the stretch run. With Thome limited by a foot injury, he managed only 17 at bats, and no home runs for the Dodgers to finish out the season.

Thome signed a one-year contract with the Twins for the 2010 season. The slugger said the new team had him feeling rejuvenated and he hit .283 with 25 home runs in 108 games. During the 2010 season, he passed Killebrew on the all-time home run list. He returned to the team on another one-year contract in 2011, hitting 12 more home runs in 71 games, including No. 600 at Detroit's Comerica Park and a 490-foot shot at Target Field that is the longest hit at the park.

With the Twins mired at the bottom of the standings, Thome agreed to waive his no-trade clause so Minnesota could deal him to Cleveland. He hit .296 in 22 games for the Indians. Thome wrapped up his career in 2012 with 30 games with the Phillies and 28 games with the Baltimore Orioles, although he didn't officially retire until August 2, 2014, when he signed a one-day contract with the Indians.

For his career, Thome had a triple slash of .276/.402/.554, while slugging 612 home runs, No. 8 on the all-time list. He added 451 doubles, 1,699 RBI and 1,747 walks. He also hit 17 home runs in 71 postseason games. His 13 walk-off home runs are the most all-time, while his 1,747 walks are seventh in big-league history. His .956 on-base plus slugging is 18th all-time, and his 2,548 strikeouts are second only to Reggie Jackson.

Thome was inducted into the Hall of Fame in 2018, and had his No. 25 retired by the Indians that same year.

Frank Viola

P, Minnesota Twins (1982-89)

H e had one of the best nicknames of any Twins pitcher, coined by a local sportswriter as "Sweet Music." And in the late 1980s there was nothing sweeter than watching the Twins ace pitch at the Metrodome.

Frank John Viola Jr. was born April 19, 1960, in East Meadow, N.Y., one of three children. He played high school baseball for East Meadow High School and was selected by the Kansas City Royals in the 16th round of the 1979 draft. He instead opted to attend St. John's University, where he pitched two years for the Redmen.

On May 21, 1981, Viola pitched against future Met Ron Darling when St. John's faced Yale University in an NCAA regional that many have called the greatest college baseball game of all time. Darling pitched 11 no-hit innings before finally allowing a hit in the 12th that scored the eventual winning run. For his part, Viola pitched 11 shutout innings before yielding to reliever Eric Stampfl in the 1-0 victory.

The Twins drafted Viola in the second round of the 1981 draft, assigning him to the Southern League's Orlando Twins. In 17 games for the AA team, Viola would finish 5-4 with 3.43 ERA. He started the 1982 season at AAA Toledo, but after eight games for the Mud Hens was promoted to Minnesota. He made his Twins debut on June 6, 1982.

Like many on that young Twins team, Viola struggled for his first years in the majors. After a 4-10 record and 5.21 ERA in 1982, he posted a 7-15 record and 5.49 ERA in 1983.

Things were looking up for Viola and the Twins in 1984. The Twins finished 81-81 on the season and were tied for first place with only a week left in the season. Viola pitched his way to an 18-12 season, with a 3.21 ERA, 10 complete games and four shutouts, finishing sixth in Cy Young voting. He again won 18 games in 1985 and followed that with 16 wins in 1986.

The Twins, of course, returned to the playoffs in 1987, winning the World Series. For his part, Viola finished with a 17-10 record and 2.90 ERA as he and teammate Bert Blyleven held together a fairly weak Twins pitching staff. In the postseason, Viola was 3-1 with a 4.31 ERA in five starts. His wins in Games 1 and 7 of the World Series garnered Viola the World Series MVP Award.

His 1988 season would be even better as Viola posted a career year. The Twins actually won more games, but fell to second place as the Oakland A's juggernaut won 104 games. The crafty southpaw finished 24-7 with a 2.64 ERA, earning his first All-Star selection and winning his only Cy Young award.

With the Twins slipping to fifth place in 1989, the team looked to ship out their star at the trade deadline. The Twins traded Viola to the New York Mets for five players, including two key parts of the 1991 World Championship squad, pitchers Rick Aguilera and Kevin Tapani. In his first full season with the Mets, Viola had his second 20-win season, finishing 20-12 with a 2.67 ERA in 1990. That was good enough for Viola's second All-Star selection and to finish in third place in Cy Young balloting. Viola started out strong again in 1991, making his third All-Star team, but finished 2-10 in the second half as the Mets collapsed.

Viola signed with the Boston Red Sox as a free agent before the 1992 season and had two solid seasons with the club before undergoing Tommy John surgery in 1994. He'd pitch only nine more major league games after that with short stints with the Cincinnati Reds and Toronto Blue Jays, retiring after the 1996 season.

For his career, Viola finished with a 176-150 record, 3.73 ERA, 74 complete games, 16 shutouts and 1,844 strikeouts in 421 games. His 112 wins as a Twin are sixth-most in team history, as are his 1,214 strikeouts. His 259 games started are No. 5 on the Twins all-time list.

Viola was inducted into the National Italian American Sports Hall of Fame in 2004 and the Twins Hall of Fame in 2005. In 2009, he was named a member of the Twins' All-Metrodome team.

Since his retirement, Viola has coached at the high school, college and pro level. His son, Frank Viola III, pitched in the White Sox and Blue Jays organizations, as well as for the St. Paul Saints.

Rube Waddell

Pitcher
Minneapolis Millers (1911-1912)
Minneapolis Bronchos (1913)
Virginia Ore Diggers (1913)

George Edward Waddell was one of the great characters of the early day of baseball. In his short 37 years of life, he dominated major league batters and frustrated teammates and managers with his off-the-field antics.

The imposing southpaw was known to miss games to go fishing or work at a fire department and to be easily distracted during games. He also developed a drinking problem during his playing days. He didn't finish school (not uncommon in those days), but was said to be literate. In the modern era, Waddell would probably have been diagnosed with some sort of disorder or developmental issues, but things were very different when it came to issues like that in those days.

He was born October 13, 1876, in Bradford, PA. His reputation as a pitching talent grew after the family moved to the town of Prospect, PA, in the early 1890s. He played for area semipro and amateur teams and, in August 1897, earned a tryout with the Pittsburgh Pirates and was apparently signed to a contract.

For reasons that appear unclear (although may have had something to do with his odd behavior), the Pirates released him before he ever played for them. Later that same year he was signed by the Louisville Colonels of the National League. He'd pitch in two games for the team, finishing 0-1 with a 3.21 ERA.

Waddell would spend most of the next two years pitching in the minor leagues before returning to Louisville to finish out the 1899 season. He posted a 7-2 record and 3.08 ERA in 10 games for the Colonels.

The Colonels were contracted before the 1900 season, but Louisville owner Barney Dreyfuss purchased half ownership of the Pirates and took 10 of his players (including Waddell) with him to his new team. He pitched in 29 games for the Pirates that year, leading the league with a 2.37 ERA while finishing with an 8-13 record. But he also established what would be a pattern throughout his career as he clashed with player/manager Fred Clarke, who suspended him for a good portion of the season. During the forced time off, Waddell pitched for semipro teams and the minor league Milwaukee Brewers, then managed by future Philadelphia Athletics skipper Connie Mack.

Waddell returned to the Pirates for the end of the 1900 season, but problems continued the following season. After only two starts, the Pirates shipped Waddell off to the Chicago Orphans in May 1901. He won 14 games for the Orphans, but after the season he signed on with a barnstorming team touring California.

For the 1902 season, he opted to join the Los Angeles Looloos of the California League. He pitched in 19 games for Los Angeles before being invited back east by his former Brewers manager Connie Mack, who was now running the Athletics.

Waddell would enjoy the greatest success of his career in Philadelphia. Although there was barely half a season left by the time Waddell joined the Athletics in 1902, he managed to pitch in 33 games. He finished the season with a 24-7 record and 2.05 ERA, while leading the American League with 210 strikeouts, while the team won the American League pennant.

He pitched for Philadelphia through the 1907 season, leading the league in strikeouts each year. His 349 strikeouts in 1904 stood as the major league record until Sandy Koufax broke it in 1965. In 1905, he led the league in wins with a 27-10 record and league-leading 1.48 ERA in 46 games. He injured his shoulder toward the end of that 1905 season while scuffling with a teammate and missed the World Series as the Athletics fell to the New York Giants in five games.

Before the 1908 season, the Athletics sold Waddell to the St. Louis Browns, another American League team. Waddell was not as effective with the Browns, but did win 19 games in 1908 and 11 games in 1909. He appeared in only 10 games for the Browns in 1910 before they released him and he finished the season with the Newark Eagles of the Eastern League.

He finished his major league career with a 193-143 record, 2,316 strikeouts and a 2.16 ERA in 407 games.

He signed with the Minneapolis Millers for the 1911 season, finishing with a 20-17 record in 54 games as the Millers won the American Association title. During that offseason, he lived on the Kentucky farm of Joe Cantillon, the Millers' manager. When floods threatened the small nearby town of Hickman, KY, on the Mississippi River, Waddell helped to stack sandbags and assisted residents when the levee broke. As a result of the wet and cold weather, he contracted pneumonia.

He returned to play for the Millers in 1912, pitching in 33 games and finishing with a 12-6 record, but continued to be weakened by his illness. During the 1912-13 offseason, he had another bout with pneumonia.

He pitched in a total of 18 games for two Northern League teams in 1913, the Minneapolis Bronchos and the Virginia Ore Diggers – reportedly drawn to the fishing on nearby Lake Vermilion – but he was a shadow of his former self.

He was diagnosed with tuberculosis and in early 1914 moved to San Antonio, TX, to be near his sister and parents. He was eventually placed in a nearby sanitarium, where he died April 1, 1914, at the age of 37.

Waddell was elected to the National Baseball Hall of Fame in 1946.

Zack Wheat

Although it's been more than 90 years since he played in a Brooklyn uniform, Zach Wheat still owns many offensive records for the storied franchise.

Wheat played for the Brooklyn Dodgers, Superbas and Robins from 1908 to 1926, and is the franchise's all-time leader in hits (2,804), games (2,322), at bats (8,859), doubles (464), triples (171) and total bases (4,003). He's among the top 10 in several other categories, including batting average, WAR, runs, RBI and walks. He was also considered one of the best defensive outfielders of his era.

Zachariah Davis Wheat was born May 23, 1888, on his family's farm near Hamilton, MO. He was the first of three sons born to Basil and Julia Wheat; all three sons would go on to play professional baseball. Middle child Mack spent seven years in the major leagues, five of those as a teammate of Zack, while youngest son Basil spent several years in the minor leagues.

After the death of Basil Sr. in 1904, the Wheats moved to Kansas City, MO, where the 16-year-old Wheat played for local semi-pro and minor league teams. In 1907, at the age of 19, he played a handful of games with the Fort Worth Panthers of the Class C Texas League. He started the 1908 season with another Texas League team, the Shreveport Pirates, before moving on to the Mobile Sea Gulls of the Class A Southern Association. He returned to Mobile in 1909 and it was during that season that the Brooklyn Superbas purchased his contract. He finished the 1909 season with Brooklyn, hitting .304 in 26 games.

In his first full season in the majors in 1910, Wheat proved to be one of the leading hitters in the National League, hitting .284 to lead the Superbas. His 172 hits, 36 doubles and 15 triples all placed among the top five in the league. He followed that up with a .287 average in 1911.

In 1912, Wheat added power to his game, hitting eight home runs, placing him among the league leaders in the Deadball Era. (The Cubs' Heinie Zimmerman led the league with 14 dingers.) He hit .305, the first of 13 .300 seasons in his career. That season he also wed his 25-year-old second cousin, Daisy Forsman; they would be married until her death in 1959.

He continued to excel for the team for the next several years. In 1916, he had one of his best seasons, hitting .312, with a league-leading .461 slugging average, and finishing among the league leaders in total bases, doubles, triples, home runs, RBI, runs and many other offensive categories. He also made his first postseason appearance that year leading the now Brooklyn Robins to the World Series. He hit only .211, though, as the Robins lost to the Boston Red Sox in five games.

In 1918, Wheat won his only batting title, hitting .335. When the Robins returned to the World Series in 1920, Wheat hit .333 in seven games, but Brooklyn still went down to the American League Champion Cleveland Indians.

As the Deadball Era drew to a close, Wheat continued to improve his offensive numbers in the 1920s. Taking advantage of the new "live ball," Wheat hit 14 home runs in 1921, his first season in double digits. Wheat followed that up with a career-high 16 home runs and 112 RBI in 1922, both in the top five for the National League. He hit for a career-high .375 average in 1923, matching that mark in 1924. At the age of 37, in 1925, Wheat hit .359 with 42 doubles, 14 triples, 14 home runs and 103 RBI.

After the 1926 season, Brooklyn released Wheat, who signed on with the Philadelphia Athletics. Wheat hit .324 in 88 games for the A's. In 1928, he signed with the Minneapolis Millers, hitting .309 in his only season in the American Association. He suffered a heel injury during the season and opted to retire at the age of 40.

During his playing career, Wheat had spent his off time as a farmer, and he turned to farming as a full-time endeavor after his retirement.

In 1932, with the Great Depression in full swing, he was forced to sell his 160-acre farm. He moved his family to Kansas City, MO, where he operated a bowling alley before becoming a police officer.

Wheat was severely injured in 1936 when he crashed his car while chasing a fugitive. After five months in the hospital, Wheat moved to Sunrise Beach, MO, where he opened a resort on Lake of the Ozarks and would spend the rest of his life.

He was elected to the Hall of Fame by the Veterans Committee in 1957 – but couldn't be inducted because he hadn't been retired the requisite 30 years. The committee voted him in again in 1959.

Wheat died of a heart attack in Sedalia, MO, in 1972.

Hoyt Wilhelm

P, Minneapolis Millers (1950-51)

When Hoyt Wilhelm played for the Minneapolis Millers, you probably wouldn't have found many observers who expected the pitcher to end up in the Hall of Fame.

He was never a highly touted prospect, he threw what had been seen as a gimmick pitch and he was already listed as 26 years old (although he was actually 27) when he made his Millers debut.

But by the time Wilhelm hung up his spikes at the age of 49, the knuckleballer had redefined the role of the baseball reliever, becoming the first to be elected to the Hall of Fame.

Wilhelm was born July 26, 1922, in Huntersville, NC, one of 11 children of a tenant farm family. He played baseball at Cornelius High School, where he began experimenting with the knuckleball – an unusual move. Before Wilhelm came along, the knuckleball was usually something an aging pitcher would throw at the end of his career in an attempt to eke out another year or two of baseball.

Wilhelm said he adopted the pitch after seeing pictures of Dutch Leonard's knuckleball grip. With his lack of velocity, Wilhelm realized developing a knuckleball was probably his best chance of having a baseball career.

He signed with the local baseball team, the Moorsville Moors of the Class D North Carolina State League in 1942, posting a 10-3 record with a 4.25 ERA in 23 games. Later that year, Wilhelm was drafted into the U.S. Army. He spent the next three years serving in Europe during World War II. He was injured in the Battle of the Bulge, receiving a Purple Heart. He played his entire career with a piece of shrapnel in his back as a result of the injury.

Wilhelm returned to the Moors after the war, winning 21 games in 1946 and 20 games in 1947. The Boston Braves purchased Wilhelm after the 1947 season, but the New York Giants drafted him from the Braves in the 1947 minor league draft that November.

The Giants assigned him to their Class B team in Knoxville, TN, in 1948. After winning 13 games there, he pitched in six games with the Class A Jacksonville Tars to finish out the season. He returned to Jacksonville in 1949, going 17-12 with a 2.66 ERA in 33 games. During his time in Jacksonville, he also met his future wife, Peggy Reeves, whom he would be married to from 1951 to his death in 2002.

His 1949 Jacksonville season was good enough to get him promoted to AAA Minneapolis for the 1950 season, where his teammates included future Hall of Fame infielder Ray Dandridge. Pitching as a starter and reliever, Wilhelm went 15-11 in 1950 and 11-14 in 1951. On May 1, 1951, he earned the opening day win for the Millers, as a young prospect by the name of Willie Mays had three hits in his Minneapolis debut.

Wilhelm was finally invited to big league camp with the Giants in 1952, 10 years after his minor league debut. Giants manager Leo Durocher was impressed enough by Wilhelm's knuckleball to add him to the roster, but sent him to the bullpen, figuring he could probably only fool batters for a few innings at a time.

He made his first appearance April 18 and on April 23 hit a home run in his first major league at bat – the only home run of his career. Wilhelm would take the league by storm, baffling batters with his knuckleball on the way to 15-3 record with a league-leading 2.43 ERA. He pitched in 71 games (all out of the bullpen), tops in the National League and a rookie record at the time. His .833 winning percentage also topped the senior circuit. He finished fourth in voting for the National League MVP award, as well as second in Rookie of the Year voting.

In 1953, he again led the league with 68 games pitched and also made his first All-Star team. He pitched his way to a 12-4 record in 1954 as the Giants won the World Series over the Cleveland Indians.

He played two more seasons for the Giants before they traded him to the St. Louis Cardinals ahead of the 1957 season. He posted a 1-4 record with a 4.25 ERA in 40 games for the Cardinals before they waived him in September, reportedly because the team's catchers were having too much trouble with his knuckleball.

The Cleveland Indians claimed him, and he pitched in two games for the team that fall. Although mostly used out of the bullpen in 1958, Wilhelm did make four starts for the Indian in his 30 games with the team. His 2-7 record (even with a 2.49 ERA), and catchers' trouble with passed balls led the Indians to let him go in August when he was claimed off of waivers by the Baltimore Orioles.

That fall he pitched in nine games for the Orioles, including four starts. On September 20, Wilhelm threw a no-hitter, beating the eventual World Champion New York Yankees 1-0. He spent most of the 1959 season in the starting rotation for the Orioles, finishing with a 15-11 record (to match the career high in wins of his rookie year) and league-leading 2.19 ERA. He also set career bests in complete games (13), shutouts (3), innings pitched (226) and strikeouts (139), while making his second All-Star team.

He split his time between the rotation and bullpen in 1960, winning 11 games. In 1961 he moved back to the bullpen, and was named to the All-Star Game in 1961 and 1962.

In January 1963 the Orioles traded the 40-year-old Wilhelm to the Chicago White Sox. He continued to excel in Chicago, saving 21 games in his first season. He set a career high with 27 saves and 73 games pitched in 1964. From 1964 to 1968, he never had an ERA over 2.00. After the Sox acquired Wilbur Wood in 1967 Wilhelm would mentor the young pitcher and helped him develop his knuckleball. Wood would win 164 games in his career, mostly with the White Sox.

In 1968, Wilhelm pitched in his 907th game, breaking Cy Young's record for games pitched. That fall the White Sox left the 46-year-old Wilhelm unprotected in the expansion draft. He was selected by the Kansas City Royals and later traded to the California Angels. He pitched in 44 games with a 2.47 ERA and 10 saves for the Angels that season. In September 1969, the Angels traded him to the Atlanta Braves, where he pitched in eight games, recording four saves and a 0.73 ERA.

He started the 1970 season with the Braves, pitching in 50 games, racking up 13 saves. On May 10, he pitched in his 1,000th game against the St. Louis Cardinals. He was also selected for his final All-Star Game. With 10 days left in the season, the Braves sold Wilhelm to the Chicago Cubs. He played in three games for the Cubs and was traded back to the Braves after the season.

Wilhelm pitched in only three games for the Braves in 1971 before they released him. He signed with the Los Angeles Dodgers in July and pitched for the team's AAA affiliate. After eight games with the Spokane Indians – managed by future Dodgers skipper Tommy Lasorda – Wilhelm joined the big league club, where he pitched in nine games.

Wilhelm pitched in 16 games for the Dodgers in 1972 before they released him on July 21, 1972, days short of his 50th birthday (although it was believed by most to be his 49th birthday).

He finished his career with a 143-122 record, 2.52 ERA and 228 saves. His 1,070 games pitched and 651 games finished were the most in major league history at the time of his retirement. He was the first player to record more than 200 career saves.

After his retirement, Wilhelm managed for two years in the Braves minor league system. He followed that with more than 20 years as a minor league coach with the Yankees organization.

After eight years of waiting, he was elected to the Hall of Fame in 1985. Wilhelm was the first relief pitcher elected to the Hall and paved the way for future relief specialists such as Rollie Fingers, Bruce Sutter, Goose Gossage and Dennis Eckersley.

He lived in Sarasota, Florida, for several years and died there in 2002 at the age of 80.

Ted Williams

OF, Minneapolis Millers (1938)

Widely regarded as the greatest hitter that ever lived, Ted Williams was a star from the moment he stepped on a baseball diamond.

Theodore Samuel Williams was born August 30, 1918, in San Diego. He was taught to throw a ball by his maternal uncle, Saul Venzor, a former semipro baseball player. He spent much of his childhood on the local fields. He was a star pitcher and hitter at San Diego's Herbert Hoover High School, as well as playing American Legion baseball.

Before he even graduated from high school, he signed with the local minor league team, the San Diego Padres of the Pacific Coast League. In 42 games in the summer of 1936, he hit .271 for the Padres.

After returning to high school for his senior year, Williams had offers from multiple major league teams, but opted to return to the Padres in 1937. As the Padres won the PCL title, Williams hit .291 with 23 home runs, 24 doubles and a .504 slugging average.

During that 1937 season, Williams caught the eye of Boston Red Sox General Manager Eddie Collins. In December of that year, the Red Sox acquired Williams for $35,000 cash and four players. Williams went to spring training with the Sox, where he met the great hitter Roger Hornsby, who was working as a batting coach. Hornsby batted over .400 three and times and was at that time the only player to twice win the Triple Crown in the major leagues – a mark that Williams would later match.

Williams hit .326 during spring training in 13 games, but the team decided he needed another year of minor league seasoning, and sent him to Minneapolis to play for the Millers in 1938. Reportedly, the Red Sox, especially manager Joe Cronin, felt Williams need to mature and get his head right.

Williams dominated the American Association in his lone season with the team, winning the league's Triple Crown with a .366 batting average, 43 home runs and 142 RBI. He also fell in love with Minnesota, enjoying the fishing and hunting in the state. He would continue to return to the state in the offseason even after he joined the Red Sox in 1939. In the fall of 1938 he met future wife Doris Soule – the daughter of a fishing guide – and would find another reason to come back to Minnesota.

In fact, Williams was duck hunting in Minnesota when news broke of the Japanese attack on Pearl Harbor, and he registered for the draft in Minnesota's Hennepin County.

But before that, Williams would make his Red Sox debut. The 20-year-old hit .327 with 32 home runs, 44 doubles and a league-leading and rookie-record 145 RBI. He walked 107 times and posted a .436 on-base percentage and .609 slugging average, while leading the league with 344 total bases. The new Sox star finished fourth in voting for the American League MVP award.

He followed that up in 1940 by improving his average to .344, while leading the league with a .442 on-base percentage. His power numbers dropped, though, as he hit 23 home runs with 113 RBI. He scored a league-leading 134 runs and had his first of 18 All-Star seasons. He would be an All-Star in every full season (and many partial) he played for the rest of his career.

His 1941 season was one for the record books. Williams hit .406 to lead the American League – a mark that still stands as the last .400 season in baseball. He also had an astounding .553 on-base percentage, while also leading the league with 135 runs, 37 home runs, 147 walks and a .735 slugging average. His OBP stood as a record until Barry Bonds broke the record in 2002. Williams still finished second in voting for the American League MVP award to Joe DiMaggio, who that season hit in a record 56 straight games.

He followed that up with another standout season in 1942, winning the American League Triple Crown with a .356 average, 36 home runs and 137 RBI. His 141 runs, 145 walks, .499 on-base percentage, .648 slugging average and 338 total bases all led the American League. He again finished second in voting for the MVP award, this time to the Yankees' Joe Gordon.

During that 1942 season, Williams joined the Naval Reserves, but received mounting criticism from some for not serving in active duty. As the sole supporter of his mother, Williams was exempt from service. Still, he went on active duty in 1943 and would miss the next three seasons serving as a pilot and instructor as a second lieutenant in the Marine Corps.

He received his discharge in January 1946 and returned to the Red Sox for the 1946 season. Williams picked up where he left off, hitting .342 with 38 home runs and 123 RBI, while leading the league in runs (142), walks (156), on-base percentage (.497) and slugging (.667).

Williams won his first MVP award that year as he led the Red Sox to their first World Series appearance since 1918. He hit .200 with one RBI as the Red Sox lost the series to the St. Louis Cardinals in seven games. It would be the only postseason appearance for The Splendid Splinter in his 19 seasons.

Williams would continue to pace the league in hitting for the next several years, winning a Triple Crown in 1947, and another batting title in 1948, while frequently topping the junior circuit in runs, walks, slugging and more. He won his second MVP award in 1949, leading the league with a career-high 43 home runs and 159 RBI, while narrowly missing out on his third Triple Crown with a .343 average, just one-ten thousandth of a point behind George Kell.

In 1950, he had already hit 25 home runs when he broke his left arm in the All-Star Game and missed most of the rest of the season. He returned in 1951, although he hit "only" .318, but still slugged 30 home runs and 126 RBI, again leading the league with 144 walks and a .464 on-base percentage. He also hit his 300th home run that season.

As the Korean War escalated in 1952, Williams was recalled to active duty as a pilot. He played in only six games that season. After being trained on the new jet airplanes, Williams would fly 39 combat missions in 1952 and 1953. He returned to the Red Sox to finish out the 1953 season, hitting .407 in 37 games.

He broke his collarbone in spring training before the 1954 season, limiting him to 117 games on the season. His .345 average would have been good enough to win the batting title if he'd had the requisite number of at bats. His .513 on-base percentage and 136 walks paced the American League.

Williams "retired" after the 1954 season, but it was largely seen as a negotiating tactic to protect his earnings as he went through a divorce with his first wife. He was offered the chance to manage the Red Sox, but declined. He signed a contract to return to the field in May 1955, and hit .356 in 98 games. He played in 136 games in 1956, the most in five years, as he hit .345 with a league-leading .479 on-base percentage. He hit 24 home runs, including No. 400 on July 17.

He again chased .400 as a 38-year-old in 1957, finishing the season with a league-leading .388 average, the second-highest of his career, along with a .526 on-base percentage and .731 slugging average. Williams won one more batting title in 1958, hitting .328, some 16 points below his career batting average.

Williams developed a stiff neck in spring training in 1959, which hindered him throughout the season. In his worst year as a hitter, Williams hit .254 – his only sub-.300 season – in 103 games. With the 1959 season leaving a bad taste in his mouth, Williams came back for one final year in 1960. He hit .316 with a .451 on-base percentage that year, with 29 home runs, including his 500th career round-tripper. In his final at-bat on September 28, 1960, Williams hit a home run.

Williams finished his career with a .344 average, the seventh-highest of all time. His career .482 on-base percentage is the highest in baseball history. He recorded 2,654 hits, 1,798 runs, 525 doubles, 521 home runs, 1,839 RBI, 2,021 walks and a .634 slugging average, all while missing nearly five seasons for military service. At the time of his retirement, he was third all-time in home runs.

Following his retirement, Williams worked for the Red Sox in a number of capacities and endorsed sports equipment for Sears Roebuck. In 1966, he was elected to the Hall of Fame in his first season of eligibility. He devoted a portion of his induction speech to recognizing the Negro League stars who never got a chance to play in the major leagues.

Williams managed the Washington Senators from 1969 to 1971 and followed the team to Texas, managing their inaugural season as the Rangers in 1972 before leaving the franchise. He continued to be active with the Hall of Fame and the Red Sox for the rest of his life.

On November 18, 1991, President George H. W. Bush presented Williams with the Presidential Medal of Freedom, the highest civilian award in the U.S. Williams was named to the Major League Baseball All-Century team in 1999 and that same year was ranked No. 8 on The Sporting News list of Baseball's 100 Greatest Players of the 20th Century.

Williams died at the age of 83 on July 5, 2002, in Inverness, Florida, after suffering a series of strokes and congestive heart failure.

Dave Winfield

OF/DH
University of Minnesota Golden Gophers (1969-1973)
Minnesota Twins (1993-1994)

D ave Winfield could possibly be the greatest all-around athlete to come out of the state of Minnesota. Born in St. Paul in 1951, the future Hall of Famer grew up near the state capitol, raised by his mother after his parents divorced when Winfield was 3 years old.

Along with his older brother Steve, Winfield excelled at multiple sports while growing up. The brothers were teammates on the two-time state champion American Legion baseball team. The brothers also excelled at Central High School, where Steve lettered in baseball three times. Dave earned All-St. Paul and All-Minnesota honors in both baseball and basketball. Both brothers are members of the school's athletic hall of fame.

The Baltimore Orioles selected Winfield in the 40th round of baseball's amateur draft in 1969, but he opted to accept a baseball scholarship from the University of Minnesota.

At the university, Winfield excelled in both baseball and basketball. In baseball, he stood out as a pitcher and hitter, being recognized as an All-American in 1973 and earning All-Big Ten honors in 1971 and 1973. He was named the Most Outstanding Player in the 1973 College World Series. Winfield played two seasons for the Gophers basketball team and future professional coach Bill Musselman, who later called him the best rebounder he had ever coached.

Winfield was selected by the San Diego Padres with the fourth overall pick in the baseball draft following his senior season. He was also drafted by the Atlanta Hawks of the National Basketball Association and the Utah Stars of the rival American Basketball Association. And despite not having played a down of college football, the hometown Minnesota Vikings picked him in the National Football League draft.

The Padres signed Winfield and immediately promoted him to the major leagues, where he hit .277 in 56 games for San Diego. He would continue to improve over the next several seasons, developing more power and a better eye at the plate. He also began to purchase tickets to Padres games for families and children that couldn't otherwise afford to attend the game.

Winfield made his first All Star Game appearance in 1977 the first of 12 consecutive years he would be selected for the game. In 1979, he hit .308 with 34 home runs and a league-leading 118 RBI. He won his first of seven Gold Gloves and finished third in voting for the National League MVP.

After the 1980 season, Winfield signed what was then the largest free agent contract in baseball history – 10 years, $23 million – with the New York Yankees. He would continue to excel in nine seasons in New York, being selected to the All-Star Game eight times, winning five Gold Gloves and five Silver Slugger awards. He also got his first taste of postseason play as the Yankees lost the 1981 World Series to the Los Angeles Dodgers. It would be the only time the Yankees would make the playoffs during his time with the team.

Despite his success on the field, Winfield had a rocky relationship with Yankees owner George Steinbrenner. Steinbrenner frequently criticized his highly paid star in public, famously calling him "Mr. May" in comparison to Reggie Jackson's "Mr. October" moniker. Steinbrenner attempted to trade Winfield – who could block any trade as a 10-year veteran with five years with the same team – and ordered his managers to bench him or move him down in the order. Winfield missed the entire 1989 season with a back injury, further inflaming the situation.

In 1990 the trouble came to a head. An investigation into alleged gambling by Winfield found no evidence that he had bet on baseball

– but it did reveal that Steinbrenner had paid Howie Spira, a gambler with alleged connections to organized crime, $40,000 for damaging information on Winfield. Baseball commissioner Fay Vincent banned Steinbrenner from day-to-day operations for life, although the ban was lifted just two years later.

Winfield returned to the field in 1990, but after only 20 games with the Yankees accepted a trade to the California Angels in May. He hit .275 with 19 home runs and 72 RBI for the Angels and won the Sporting News Comeback Player of the Year Award. Winfield played one more season for the Angels, then signed with the Toronto Blue Jays for the 1992 season.

With the Blue Jays, Winfield had another strong season, hitting .290 with 26 home runs and 108 RBI. He won his final Silver Slugger award and finished fifth in voting for the American League MVP Award. He also returned to the postseason as the Blue Jays won the World Series in 1992, the only ring Winfield won in his career.

Once again a free agent, Winfield opted to sign a two-year deal with his hometown team before the 1993 season. The 41-year-old Winfield played in 143 games for the Twins, batting .271 with 21 home runs and 76 RBI. On September 16, he collected his 3,000th hit in a game against the Oakland Athletics.

Winfield played in 77 games for the Twins in 1994 before the players went on strike August 12. On August 31, the Twins traded him to the Cleveland Indians for a player to be named later. As the season was eventually cancelled, Twins and Indians executives settled the trade by going to dinner – with Cleveland picking up the tab.

After the 1994 season, Winfield received the Roberto Clemente Award, which recognizes the player who best exemplifies sportsmanship, community involvement and contribution to his team.

When baseball resumed for the 1995 season, Winfield signed a one-year deal with the Indians. He played in only 46 games, hitting

.191, as a rotator cuff injury kept him on the disabled list for most of the season. He retired following the season.

Winfield was ranked No. 94 on The Sporting News' list of Baseball's 100 Greatest Players in 1998. The Padres inducted him into the team's Hall of Fame in 2000 and retired his No. 31 in 2001.

He was elected to the Baseball Hall of Fame in his first year of eligibility in 2001 (with former teammate Kirby Puckett), the first Padre inducted into the hall. In 2006, he was among the first class of players inducted into the College Baseball Hall of Fame.

Carl Yastrzemski

OF, Minneapolis Millers (1960)

More than two decades after one future Boston Red Sox legend roamed the outfield for the Minneapolis Millers, another played for the team in its final season.

Carl Yastrzemski, who spent most of his career facing comparisons to the great Ted Williams, would end up forging his own Hall of Fame career which included more than 3,000 hits and 400-plus home runs.

Yastrzemski was born in Bridgehampton, NY, to Carl Yastrzemski and Hattie Skonieczny. The older Carl was a semi-pro baseball player and the younger Carl served as a batboy and, beginning at the age of 14, eventually played for the team. A number of teams scouted Yastrzemski in high school, including the Red Sox and New York Yankees. The family was also fielding a number of scholarship offers, before eventually settling on Notre Dame, where Yastrzemski attended on a baseball and basketball scholarship.

After his freshman year at Notre Dame, Yastrzemski accepted a $108,000 bonus offer from the Red Sox, signing in November 1958. The Red Sox assigned him to the Class B Raleigh Capitals of the Carolina League for the 1959 season, where Yastrzemski played second base and shortstop. He impressed at Raleigh, hitting .377 with a .472 OBP, 15 home runs and 100 RBI in 120 games.

At the end of the 1959 season, the Red Sox sent him to join the Millers for the playoffs. According to Yastrzemski's 2007 autobiography, he was immediately inserted into the lineup at shortstop in the playoff series against Omaha and scored the winning run in the 10th inning. Omaha protested his eligibility to play, though, and the teams had to replay the game the next day without Yastrzemski. The Millers won again, taking the next game as well to move on to the championship. Yastrzemski would play against Fort Worth as the Millers won the American Association title.

After winning the series, the Millers went on to play Cuba's Havana Sugar Kings, then a Cincinnati Reds farm team, in the Junior World Series. It was shortly after the Cuban revolution and the United States still had diplomatic relations, albeit tenuous, with the Castro regime. The first two games were played in freezing cold weather in Minneapolis, with the third game getting snowed out. With the cold weather, the teams agreed to finish the series in Cuba. And that's where things got interesting, as Yastrzemski wrote.

At the stadium the foul lines were marked by soldiers. There were about 3,000 troops in the park – in foul territory, behind the plate, in the stands, in the dugouts. There were more submachine guns than bats, one guy wrote. He was right.

Fidel Castro himself arrived at the game via helicopter. The former pitcher made it clear he expected the Sugar Kings to win. According to Yastrzemski, many of the players feared what would happen if the Millers prevailed. As it turned out, Havana won in seven games and the Millers made it out of Cuba alive.

The Red Sox brought Yastrzemski to spring training in 1960 and assigned him the locker next to Williams, who was nearing the end of his career. The Sox opted to send him down to Minneapolis for the season, though, so Yastrzemski could learn left field and prepare to take over for the legendary hitter.

It was the Millers' final season before they cleared out of town to make room for the Twins in 1961. Yastrzemski hit .339 for the season, just missing winning the league's batting title.

Williams did retire after the 1960 season, and on opening day 1961 it was Yastrzemski filling the legend's shoes in left field at Fenway Park. Yastrzemski turned in a solid season at the plate, hitting .266, with 31 doubles, 11 home runs and 80 RBI, although he did make 10 errors in the outfield. He followed that up in 1962 with a .296 average, 43 doubles, 19 home runs and 94 RBI.

He really broke out in 1963, making the first of his 18 All-Star Games. Yastrzemski won the American League batting title with a .321 average. He also topped the league in OBP (.418), doubles (40), hits (183) and walks (95). Yastrzemski also improved his defense, winning the first of seven Gold Gloves.

Three more strong seasons followed, before Yastrzemski had his career season in 1967. He won the triple crown, leading the American League in average (.326), home runs (44) and RBI (121) – the last two career highs. He also led the league in runs, hits, OBP, slugging and total bases, while winning the MVP award.

The Red Sox also won the American League pennant that season for the first time in more than 20 years. Yastrzemski hit .400 with three home runs as the Sox lost to the St. Louis Cardinals in seven games. Yastrzemski was selected by *Sports Illustrated* as the 1967 Sportsman of the Year.

Yastrzemski won another batting title in 1968 – the so-called "Year of the Pitcher" – with a .301 average. His 119 walks and .429 OBP also led the league. His average slipped to .255 in 1969, but Yastrzemski did hit 40 home runs with 111 RBI.

His 1970 season was almost as good as his triple crown year, as Yastrzemski barely missed winning a fourth battle title with a career-high .329 average, with 40 home runs and 102 RBI. His 125 runs, .452 OBP and .592 slugging average all topped the American League. His 23 stolen bases made him only the second player in Red Sox history to steal 20 bases and hit 20 home runs in one season.

Yastrzemski continued to be an important part of the Red Sox for the rest of the decade, helping them to their first American League East title in 1975. At the age of 35, he hit .455 as the Red Sox topped the Oakland Athletics in three games to win the American League Championship Series. He hit .310 in the seven-game World Series loss to the Reds.

On July 14, 1977, Yastrzemski recorded his 2,655th hit to pass Ted Williams as the Red Sox all-time hit leader. He hit is 400th career home run and 3,000th hit in 1979, making him the first American Leaguer to reach both marks.

Yastrzemski retired after the 1983 season, having played 23 seasons, all with the Red Sox. His 3,308 games played set a record broken by Pete Rose a year later. He finished his career with 3,419 hits, 646 doubles, 452 home runs, 1,844 RBI, 1,816 runs, 1,845 walks, a .285 batting average, .379 on-base percentage and .462 slugging average.

He was elected to the Hall of Fame in 1989, and the Red Sox retired his No. 8 that same season. In 1999, Yastrzemski was ranked No. 72 on *The Sporting News* list of the 100 Greatest Baseball Players and was also a finalist for the Major League Baseball All-Century Team.

APPENDIX

M innesota was also home to several other famous figures that may not have achieved their greatest renown for playing profession-ally in the state. Instead, these hockey, football, basketball, political fig-ures – and one comic strip star – stand out for some other reason. Still, it's interesting to note their Minnesota connections.

Walter Alston

The Hall of Fame manager of the Brooklyn and Los Angeles Dodgers (1954-76) won 2,040 games and four World Series titles. He managed the St. Paul Saints in 1948 and 1949.

Herb Brooks

Coached the U.S Olympic Hockey team to a gold medal in the "Miracle on Ice" 1980 Winter Olympics and silver in 2002. Won three NCAA hockey championships at the University of Minnesota. Played baseball for the St. Paul Minnesota Mining and Manufacturing (3M) team, as well as high school ball.

Charlie Brown

Let's just assume that the Peanuts gang lives in Minnesota, since creator Charles Schultz creator was from St. Paul. In a 1954 comic strip, it's established that the kids live in Hennepin County, and 1960s and 1970s specials show St. Paul, though some later strips and specials indicate a California location.

Chief Bender

A member of the Ojibwe tribe, Bender was born in Crow Wing County. He won 212 games as a pitcher and was elected to the Hall of Fame in 1953. Bender is credited by some as inventing the slider.

Charles Comiskey

Comiskey purchased the Western League's Sioux City team in 1894, moving it to St. Paul for the 1895 season as the St. Paul Apostles. After serving as player/manager for five seasons, moved the team to

Chicago. Comiskey would be owner of the White Sox until his death in 1931. He was elected to the Hall of Fame as an executive in 1939.

Carm Cozza

Cozza was the head football coach at Yale University from 1965 to 1996, winning 179 games and 10 Ivy League titles. He was elected to the College Football Hall of Fame in 2002. He played town ball for several communities in Minnesota throughout the 1950s.

Leo Durocher

The Hall of Fame manager won 2,008 games in his career for the Brooklyn Dodgers, New York Giants, Chicago Cubs and Houston Astros. Won four World Series titles as a player, coach and manager. Played the 1927 season for the St. Paul Saints. Elected to the Hall of Fame in 1994.

Jimmie Foxx

The first baseman was the second player in major league history to hit 500 home runs (after Babe Ruth), finishing his career with 534 home runs and a .325 average. Spent the 1958 season as a coach for the Minneapolis Millers. Elected to the Hall of Fame in 1951.

Bud Grant

The Hall of Fame football coach won 158 games and coached in three Super Bowls as coach of the Minnesota Vikings. Before his coaching career, Grant lettered in football, basketball and baseball at the University of Minnesota. Played for the Minneapolis Lakers basketball team from 1949 to 1951 and continued to play town ball during the offseason.

Morley Jennings

The College Football Hall of Fame Coach won 153 games in the early 1900s. Played for the Minneapolis Millers from 1915-22.

Roger Maris

Maris hit 275 home runs, including a record-setting 61 in 1961. He won the American League MVP award in 1960 and 1961, was a seven-time All Star and won three World Series. Born in Hibbing in 1934.

Eugene McCarthy

Before McCarthy was a member of the U.S. House of Representatives, a U.S. Senator and frequent presidential candidate, the Minnesota native played baseball at St. John's University in Collegeville and for the Watkins town ball team.

Minnie Minoso

Minoso played in the Cuban, Mexican, Negro and major leagues, racking up more than 2,000 hits across the various leagues. A member of the Mexican, Hispanic and Cuban baseball Halls of Fame, he made two stunt appearance for the St. Paul Saints, taking one at-bat in 1993 and 2003, making him the first player to play professionally in seven different decades.

Satchel Paige

The Negro League star, who made his major-league debut in 1948 at the age of 42, was elected to the baseball Hall of Fame in 1971. Paige made several exhibition appearances in Minnesota on various traveling teams.

Jim Pollard

Pollard played eight seasons for the Minneapolis Lakers of the NBA, winning five titles. He played for Jordan's town ball team during the offseason. Elected to the basketball Hall of Fame in 1978.

Tubby Raymond

Another town ball player in Minnesota, Raymond also won 300 games as the head football coach at the University of Delaware. Elected to the College Football Hall of Fame in 2003.

Swede Risberg

Famous not so much for what he did on the diamond, but off it, Risberg was a member of the 1919 "Black Sox" team that threw the World Series. Banned from baseball along with seven other players, Risberg continued to play for several semi-pro teams throughout the Midwest. In 1923 and 1924, he played for the Rochester Aces. When he died at age 81 in 1975, he was the last living Black Sox player.

BIBLIOGRAPHY

Anderson, David, ed., *Before the Dome* (Minneapolis, MN: Nodin Press, 1993)

Aschburner, Steve, *The Good, The Bad & The Ugly* (Chicago, IL: Triumph Books, 2008)

Aschburner, Steve, *Harmon Killebrew: Ultimate Slugger* (Chicago, IL: Triumph Books, 2012)

Baylor, Don, with Claire Smith, *Don Baylor* (New York, NY: St, Martin's Press, 1989)

Bernstein, Ross, *Batter-Up: Celebrating a Century of Minnesota Baseball* (Minneapolis, MN: Nodin Press, 2002)

Butler, Hal, *The Bob Allison Story* (New York, NY: Simon & Schuster, 1967)

Campanella, Roy, *It's Good to be Alive* (Lincoln, NE: University of Nebraska Press, 1995)

Conklin, Carroll C., *Twins Heroes* (Bright Stone Press, 2013)

Doeden, Matt, *The Negro Leagues* (Minneapolis, MN: Millbrook Press, 2017)

Freedman, Lew, *Knuckleball* (New York, NY: Sports Publishing, 2015)

Gomez, Vernona and Lawrence Goldstone, *Lefty: An American Odyssey* (New York, NY: Ballantine Books, 2012)

Grant, Jim, with Tom Sabellico and Pat O'Brien, *The Black Aces: Baseball's Only African-American Twenty-Game Winners* (Farmingdale, NY: Marathon Press, 2006)

Grow, Douglas, *We're Gonna Win Twins!* (Minneapolis, MN: University of Minnesota Press, 2010)

Hamann, Rex, *The Minneapolis Millers of the American Association* (Charleston, SC: Arcadia Publishing, 2015)

Henninger, Thom, *Tony Oliva: The Life & Times of a Minnesota Twins Legend* (Minneapolis, MN: University of Minnesota Press, 2015)

Hirsch, James S., *Willie Mays: The Life, The Legend* (New York: Scribner, 2010)

Hoffbeck, Steven R., ed., *Swinging for the Fences: Black Baseball in Minnesota* (St. Paul, MN: Minnesota Historical Society Press, 2005)

Hrbek, Kent, with Dennis Brackin, *Kent Hrbek's Tales from the Minnesota Twins Dugout* (Champaign, IL: Sports Pub., 2007)

Irvin, Monte with Phil Pepe, *Few and Chosen: Defining Negro League Greatness* (Chicago, IL: Triumph Books, 2007)

Irvin, Monte, with James A. Riley, *Nice Guys Finish First: The Autobiography of Monte Irvin* (New York: Carroll & Graf Publishers, 1996)

Jaffe, Jay, *The Cooperstown Casebook* (New York, NY: St. Martin's Press, 2017)

Kaat, Jim, *Still Pitching* (Chicago, IL: Triumph Books, 2003)

Kahn, Roger, *The Era 1947-1957: When the Yankees, the Giants, and the Dodgers Ruled the World* (New York, NY: Diversion Books, 2012)

Karlen, Neal, *Slouching Toward Fargo* (St. Paul, MN: Minnesota Historical Society Press, 1999)

Klima, John, *The Game Must Go On* (New York, NY: St. Martin's Press, 2015)

Mays, Willie with Lou Sahadi, *Say Hey: The Autobiography of Willie Mays* (New York, NY: Simon & Schuster, 1988)

Montville, Leigh, *Ted Williams* (New York, NY: Doubleday, 2004)

Neary, Kevin, with Leigh A. Tobin, *Closer* (Philadelphia, PA: Running Press, 2013)

Niekro, Phil and Joe, with Ken Picking, *The Niekro Files: The Uncensored Letters of Baseball's Most Notorious Brothers* (Chicago, IL: Contemporary Books, 1988)

Nowlin, Bill, *Ted Williams at War* (Cambridge, MA: Rounder Books, 2007)

Peterson, Armand and Tom Tomashek, *Town Ball: The Glory Days of Minnesota Amateur Baseball* (Minneapolis, MN: University of Minnesota Press, 2006)

Puckett, Kirby, and Mike Bryan, *I Love This Game! My Life and Baseball* (New York, NY: HarperCollins Publishers, 1993)

Riley, James A., *The Biographical Encyclopedia of the Negro Baseball Leagues* (New York: Caroll & Graf Publishers, 1994)

Riley, James A., *Dandy, Day, and the Devil* (Cocoa, FL: TK Publishers, 1987)

Smith, Ron, *The Sporting News Selects Baseball's 100 Greatest Players* (St. Louis, MO: The Sporting News Publishing Co., 1998)

Sullivan, Bill, *Long Before the Miracle* (CreateSpace, 2016)

Swift, Tom, *Chief Bender's Burden* (Lincoln, NE: University of Nebraska Press, 2008)

Thornley, Stew, *Baseball in Minnesota* (St. Paul, MN: Minnesota Historical Society Press, 2006)

Thornley, Stew, *The St. Paul Saints* (St. Paul, MN: Minnesota Historical Society Press, 2015)

Urdahl, Dean, *Touching Bases with our Memories: The Players Who Made the Twins 1961-2001* (St. Cloud, MN: North Star Press of St. Cloud, 2001)

Wendel, Tim, *Down to the Last Pitch* (Boston, MA: Da Capo Press, 2014)

White, Frank M., *They Played for the Love of the Game: Untold Stories of Black Baseball in Minnesota* (St. Paul, MN: Minnesota Historical Society Press, 2016)

Yastrzemski, Carl, *Yastrzemski* (New York, NY: Rugged Land, LLC, 2007)

About the Author

Jonathan Sweet is an award-winning journalist who lives in Minneapolis with his wife, two exceptional children and one fairly dim-witted dog.

Read more at https://brickpicklemedia.com/.

Made in the USA
Monee, IL
19 July 2023

38939018R10111